Art of the Dogfight
Volume 1

Jim Wilberg, M.D.

For Anne Marie, who kept the faith.

Acknowledgements

Color aircraft profiles © Bob Pearson. Purchase his CD of WWI aircraft profiles for $50 US/ Canadian, 40 €, or £30, airmail postage included, via Paypal to Bob at: bpearson@kaien.net

For our aviation books, please see our website at: www.aeronautbooks.com.

I am looking for photographs of the less well-known German aircraft of WWI to complete this series. For questions or to help with photographs you may contact me at jherris@me.com.

Interested in WWI aviation? Join The League of WWI Aviation Historians (**www.overthefront.com**), Cross & Cockade International (**www.crossandcockade.com**), and Das Propellerblatt (**www.propellerblatt.de**).

ISBN: 978-1-953201-25-6
Design and layout: Jack Herris
Cover design: Aaron Weaver
Digital photo editing: Jack Herris

Books for Enthusiasts by Enthusiasts
www.aeronautbooks.com

2

Above: Jim Dietz's two paintings, *Bonne Chance* (front endpaper) and *C'est le Guerre* (back endpaper) are wonderfully evocative pieces depicting the start of and the return of a sortie by a British squadron in the First World War. The details are superb, and for the observant reader, a story is visually told.

Above: Line up of Sopwith Camels, No. 10 sqdn., RNAS, Bray Dunes aerodrome, 4th February 1918.

Above: F/2Lt. W.H. Wilmot in his "B" flight Camel.

Above: A modern replica Sopwith Camel depicted in the black and white stripes of "A" flight; "B" flight had red and white stripes and "C" flight had blue and white stripes.

Below: Computer image of a conceptualized line up of "B" flight camels in February/March 1918 by Mark Miller.

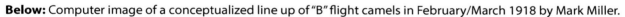

Above: Lt. Kurt Katzenstein in his Pfalz D.IIIa, black fuselage. Note signal pistol attached to top wing, indicating he would lead his flight.

Above: Lt. Holthusen's Pfalz D. IIIa draws a lot of attention. Note that the national insignia has been converted to the 1918 style by this point in time, May, 1918.

Art of the Dogfight Volume 1 Table of Contents

Cover Painting: Bolt From the Blue

My friend, renowned aviation artist Jim Dietz created this painting especially for the cover of *Art Of The Dogfight*. It depicts an offensive patrol flight of Sopwith Camels from B flight, 10 Squadron RNAS engaging a kette of Pfalz DIII fighters of Royal Prussian Jasta 30 in Feb or March, 1918. This painting exemplifies the author's concept of "visual history" in that the aircraft are portrayed as accurately as possible, and that research would indicate that these two fighter formations were indeed opposite from each other on the Western front at the time depicted, thanks to research by Greg van Wyngarden and Bruno Schmalling.

It is the extensive collaboration between the aviation historians and the aviation artist that gives rise to the creation of visual history for us to enjoy and learn from.

8

Acknowledgements

This book project began over 25 years ago. It was started during a conversation I had with my good friend Charlie Woolley while sitting over coffee and bagels at his spectacular summer home located in the Midcoast of Maine. He was kind and encouraging. Since he had several large, authoritative books already in print on several subjects to his credit, I took his positive words as the impetus to get started.

Because of his own experience and book-writing wisdom, I think Charlie is not surprised that it has taken these 25 years to actually complete the book! Nearly every summer, we would meet and talk and he would continue to stay positive towards my book project as it slowly evolved. Thank you Charlie, you are not only a friend, but an inspiration to all of us mere amateur First World War aviation historians.

Since the premise of the book is the first 100 years of First World War Aviation art and the stories behind the visual history that those pieces of artwork tell in visual format, I owe a nearly unmeasurable amount of gratitude to the aviation artists who enthusiastically helped in this book.

I would refer the reader to the end of volume 4, where a special section of artists biographies is located and where there is a cross-reference by page number for the reader to help locate the images of an individual artist as they appear in the book. It is here also that the details of permission to use the artwork in the book is detailed.

It should not need to be stated: however all the artwork in this book is copyrighted by the artist and cannot be reproduced without the proper permission being obtained by the artist or by the proper authority representing the artist.

Sadly, many of the artists that I was so blessed to communicate with and grow to know during the research for this book have "gone west". Fortunately, there are still exceptionally talented aviation artists who are to this day creating evocative, spectacular aviation art for our enjoyment.

In the artist biography section is also included, when possible, the current means of connecting with these modern aviation artists. I would heartily recommend any reader to contact their favorite artist in order to buy some of their available artwork or even to commission a special piece. We, who enjoy the study of aviation history and enjoy aviation art, must continue to be supportive of these artists in any way we can.

These four volumes represent my 9th–12th book

in print and along the way, I feel truly blessed to have had such exceptional support from my friends and fellow first world war aviation historians: most of whom, I freely admit, have a depth of experience and knowledge that I cannot begin to emulate. It is because of their generous answering of my frequent questions and the kind sharing of the results of their hard work and their tireless efforts and their incredible research that allows many of the details of these stories to be told in these volumes.

One of the most obvious and profound changes to our world is the internet, which allows for the rapid sharing of thoughts, observations, photos and other historical insights that helped go into this book. This modern innovation has been of tremendous value in keeping close contact with my associates in the study of First World War aviation history, no matter where they are in the world.

From Canada, Stewart Taylor and Edward Peter Soye have been very helpful. From Belgium, the expert of anything concerning the Belgian AIr Service in WWI, Walter Pieters has kindly made his work available to me. From France Bruno Couplez, Bernard Klaeyle and David Mechin have been all invaluable to me over the course of several books now. From Italy, Gregory Alegi, Andrea Angiolino, Mauro Antonellini, and Paolo Varriale have likewise been stalwart supporters over several books, including this one.

From Germany, Dieter Groschel, M.D. and Bruno Schmaling have been extremely helpful. From England, Alex Revell and Ray Rimell have been like professors to me, their knowledge of WWI aviation history seems to be limitless.

There were also many fellow members of the Cross and Cockade Society, who over the previous decades have shared their particular knowledge of a subject and/ or photos in a very open and supportive manner.

From "down under", Adrian Hellwig and Colin Owers were very forthcoming with any help that I requested from them. Richard Alexander of Wingut Wings was simply super in his efforts to help acquire some of the more unusual photographs from their collection.

Here in the United States I have been so blessed by the support of numerous historians, without their insights and knowledge this compilation of so many varied topics of First World War Aviation history would not have been possible. All here were critical in this book: Javier Arango, Lance Bronnenkant, Jay

Broze, Ross Fenn, Dennis Gordon, Peter Grosz, Jon Guttman, Ted Hamady, Jack Hunter, Peter Kilduff, Jim Miller, Mike O'Neal, Steven Ruffin, Stephen Skinner, Steve Suddaby, Alan Toelle, Charlie Woolley and (far from last by any measure) Greg van Wyngarden.

Since this endeavor took more than several decades, I might have inadvertently left out the name of someone who helped along the way. If so, please accept my apologies and my sincere thanks for having provided that assistance when you did.

I would especially like to thank my friend and publisher Jack Herris. Because of his assistance and direction, my previous books and these four volumes are possible. Without his expertise and without the phenomenal, almost magical talents of Aaron Weaver as well at Aeronautbooks these books would not exist. To both Jack and Aaron you have obviously earned my deepest and most sincere thanks for all that you do on my behalf. Also know that I remain in awe at the near encyclopedic knowledge you both have of this subject matter.

Finally, there are less than a handful of images used in these two volumes for which I could not, in the end, assign attribution. I include them here because I think they add tremendous value to the book and I add them here in humble respect to the artists who I feel that their talents deserve to be included with their peers. If anyone can help the author to find the proper attribution, please contact aeronautbooks and we will work on adding any correction going forward as possible.

If there are errors in the text, they are not because of all the wonderful support during the past 25 years that I have had from the people mentioned above, any errors are the authors.

Jim WIlberg

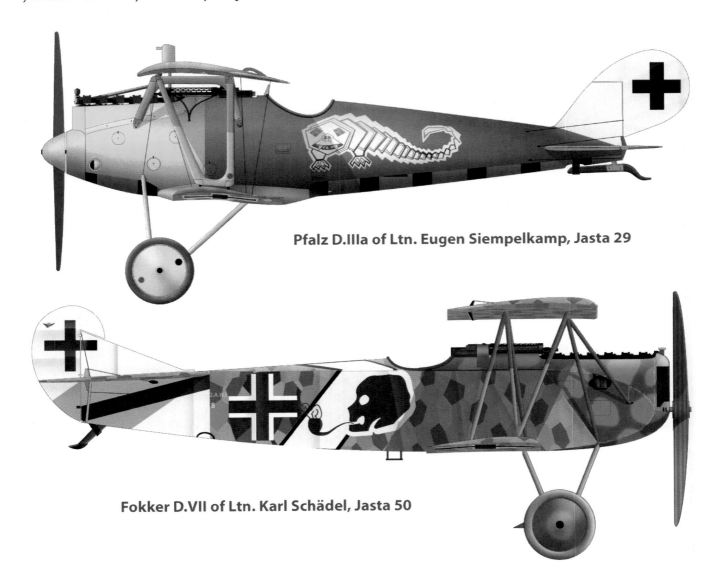

Pfalz D.IIIa of Ltn. Eugen Siempelkamp, Jasta 29

Fokker D.VII of Ltn. Karl Schädel, Jasta 50

Foreword

I was much honored to be asked to write a foreword to Jim Wilberg's amazing *Art of the Dogfight* series. Jim and I have been colleagues in the field of WWI aviation historical research for many years. We also share a passion for finding and sharing great art that deals with our favorite subject. There is no one better qualified to write this series of volumes dedicated to WWI aero art than Jim Wilberg.

By the time that the Great War broke out in 1914, black and white photography was a highly advanced art. Historians are fortunate to have a wealth of monochrome photographs documenting the aircraft and airmen of the First World War, by both professional and amateur photographers. Air-to-air photographs of airplanes in flight are less common than images of these craft on the ground, but there are still thousands of such images – many taken by observer-photographers during training. Photos of actual aerial combat are, however, extremely rare. Only a handful of such photos are known, and some are of dubious authenticity. The infamous 'Cockburn-Lange' photos of British and German aircraft in combat were long considered to be genuine wartime photos but have since been revealed as a hoax perpetrated with models and camera tricks. The fabled French ace Georges Guynemer did succeed in having a special camera fitted to some of his SPAD fighter planes; he managed to expose a few blurry photos of German aircraft that he was attacking, but in general the gun cameras of WWII were far in the future. Similarly, color photography existed but was still in the developmental stage. There are only a few dozen grainy period color photos of WWI aircraft known, most created by French and British photographers using the autochrome process.

Thus, we have generally had to rely on visual artists for images of what aerial combat looked like in 1914–1918. This was realized during the war, and painters from many nations produced illustrations of military aviation – these included official military artists and those who produced work for the illustrated magazines of the day. Some were commissioned as war artists who went to the front (and flew over it) and interacted with the airmen in order to produce an historical record. Frenchman Henri Farré is the most famous of these; he pioneered the new art of portraying warfare in three dimensions and created memorable images of airborne heroics. Among the British war artists, Joseph Simpson painted many iconic scenes and the brothers Robert and Sydney Carline (both of whom actually flew in action) produced paintings for the Imperial War Museum. Of the eight official US war artists, Capt. Harry Townsend produced the most images of American aviation, having spent time at the First Pursuit Group.

Mention should also be made of a very select group of men who were primarily combat airmen but who used their artistic talents in order to record their own experiences and those of their comrades. The American Clayton Knight is the most familiar of these; he flew D.H.9's in the RAF, and later became a very successful commercial artist who illustrated many WWI aviation books of the 1930's. The German fighter ace Rudolf Stark, American ace Lansing Holden, and the British airmen Roderic Hill and Sir Robert Saundby (both of whom later rose to very high rank) also contributed to the pictorial record.

Interest in such art waned after the war, but was revived with the advent of the aviation-oriented "pulp magazines" of the 1930's. These magazines often featured gaudy cover paintings depicting Fokkers, Spads, and many other types in spectacular combat. However, the world events of 1939 crowded WWI aircraft from the pulps in favor of more contemporary topics, and the airplanes and aviators of the Great War faded into irrelevance for many years.

Interest in WWI aviation – and associated art – began to revive in the late 1950's. New, commercially available model kits of aircraft of the era (both flying models and plastic scale kits) inspired a new wave of fascination for the topic, and spurred research into accurate colors and structural details. The magazine *Model Airplane News* regularly featured evocative cover paintings of WWI planes by the prolific Jo Kotula, who would also produce art for plastic model box tops. Similar British magazines like *Aero Modeller* also featured WWI aircraft cover paintings by respected illustrators. In the early 1960's, the Leach Corporation marketed a series of superb full color prints in its "Heritage of the Air" series, created by Merv Corning. These iconic prints were among the first to have well-researched, accurate depictions of specific events from aviation history, and they inspired many other artists such as James Deneen and Bob Carlin to produce their own WWI aero art. At about the same time, Jack Leynnwood, Brian Knight, and Roy Cross began producing magnificent box top art of WWI and II airplanes for model kits. These would all help to inspire a new generation of WWI aviation enthusiasts, artist and historians.

Both Jim Wilberg and this writer grew up in 1960's, and we share many memories of iconic artworks that influenced our youthful minds to go along similar paths. We both cite the significant impact of Joseph A. Phelan's superbly designed and illustrated 1966 book, *Heroes and Aeroplanes of the Great War1914–1918.* It is a wonderfully produced treasure trove of the author/illustrator's own drawings and watercolors along with a lively text. This was soon followed by *Illustrated History of World War I in the Air* in 1971; edited by Stanley M. Ulanoff, it presented the classic work of Farré and Clayton Knight, alongside works by Phelan and the best of the model boxtop artists to a new audience. In many ways, Jim Wilberg's new *Art of the Dogfight* volumes are direct successors to those influential books, and I am sure that Jim's books will have similar impact on today's readers.

Somehow, in addition to his busy medical career, Jim Wilberg has spent years researching and acquiring WWI aviation art and building relationships with many of today's best aero artists; besides this he is also an accomplished historian and writer. He has already produced three magnificent books from Aeronaut showcasing the art of the impressive triumvirate of Russell Smith, James Dietz, and Steve Anderson. Jim has also written biographies of Jean Navarre and Gottfried Banfield. *The Art of the Dogfight*, however, is his magnum opus – a dream project that he has been working toward for many years. In these volumes, each superb piece of art is accompanied by Jim's description of the history behind the painting, as well as relevant photos. In these combined volumes, the reader is presented with a virtual history of the air war of 1914–1918 accompanied by some of the best aviation art from the past and present. Jim is to be heartily congratulated on writing and presenting such a valuable compilation and to Jack Herris for having the foresight to edit and publish his work. I know these books will have a valued spot on my bookshelves for many years to come.

Greg VanWyngarden

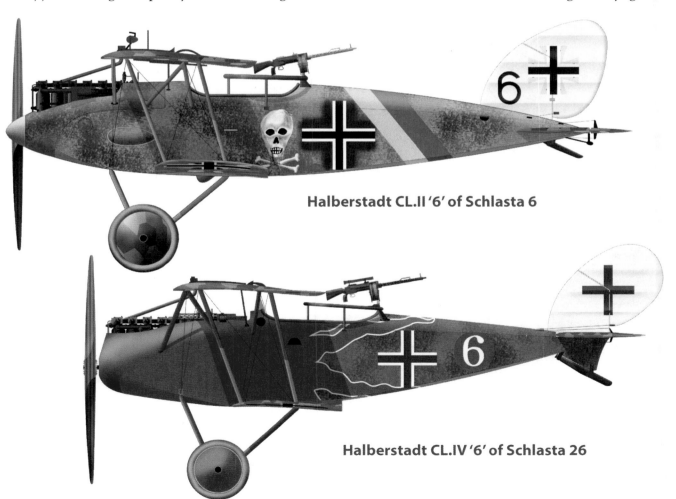

Halberstadt CL.II '6' of Schlasta 6

Halberstadt CL.IV '6' of Schlasta 26

Introduction

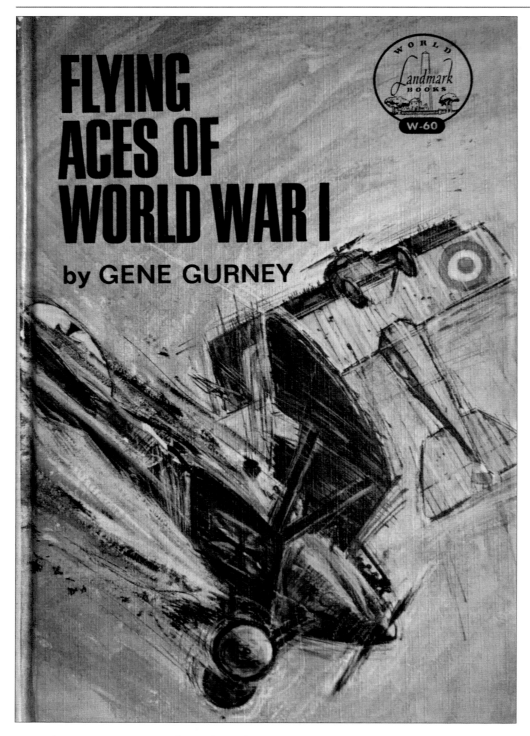

Left: Cover that began my interest. Francis Chauncy

As long as I can remember, I have been interested in the stories of aviation during the First World War. I can best date the beginning of my interest to a book, *Flying Aces of WWI*, written by Gene Gurney, published by Random House in 1965 and given to me by my father in July of that year for my ninth birthday. I can recall reading and re-reading the brief biographies of the pilots that were in the book. I would often pause in my reading to look at the book's cover (by Francis A. Chauncy), in order to

Above: Cover Art from *Aircraft and Flyers of the First World War* by Joseph Phelan.

have that dramatic visual image enhance the mental images that were developing in my mind as I read the words in the book's text.

And then, for next year's birthday, I received Thomas Funderburk's *The Fighters* (Grossett and Dunlap, 1965). And I was hooked on the subject of First World War aviation history for good. His writing was incredible: now names from history were actual people to me. Funderburk"s skill was to make the aviators seem present, very much alive. His respect for these first aviators was very clear, and the personal touches of their stories that he brought to his writings made their stories that much better, that much more real to the reader. From the back dust-cover:

"Such research is the making of *The Fighters*: not an attempt to exhaust the subject, but a colorfully representative picture of the men and planes of World War I."

Even now, my copy of that book sits on my desk as I write and i read sections from time to time

Illustrated History of World War I in The Air

Stanley Ulanoff

Right: Another cover art example by Joseph Phelan.

Above: Renwal model airplane kit, Spad XIII of American ace David Putnam.

in the hope that I can somehow match what he accomplished (although I must be honest to myself and acknowledge that I fall short too often).

Over fifty years have passed since those first two books, and now my personal library consists of more than 300 books and hundreds of journals concerning the study of First World War aviation. In my study of the subject, I seem to never lose or forget that initial interest in the study of those first military pilots and of the aircraft that they so bravely flew during the war.

Over the years, I developed a firm belief that artwork concerning the pilots, their aircraft and their missions could tell a history of the subject in a very unique, vivid, and compelling manner.

Looking again on the cover jacket illustration of *Aircraft and Flyers of the First World War* by Joseph A.Phelan (Grosset and Dunlap,1973) I can see Mr.Phelan's meticulous use of his research in bringing to his artwork as accurate a depiction of the combat action as possible.

The viewer can easily see the enormous size of the German Staaken night bomber, the much

smaller British Sopwith night-fighters making their attacks, with Phelan accurately portraying the Sopwith fighters having special markings and special armaments. Phelan's image thus gives us a uniquely visual and historic reference in a way that text or photos cannot..

Stanley Ulanoff produced an interesting book, *Illustrated History of World War I in the Air* (Arco, 1971) which utilized artwork by different artists to tell very brief stories associated with the pilot and/ or plane featured in the artwork. The book jacket illustration is by none other than Joseph Phelan and it depicts the flamboyant French ace Jean Navarre in his red-colored Nieuport 16 in one of the air combats, that would lead to the first time a French aviator had downed two German aircraft in a single day.

Once again, telling the story in a "visual-historical" contex; Phelan accurately depicts the type of aircraft and its markings. To my knowledge, this was the only book to have attempted to utilize aviation art to help tell the history of military aviation in the FIrst World War since several books

Above: Poster of WWI Aces from Renwal models, circa late 1960's.

were produced in the 1920s(please refer to chapter concerning aviator artists).

Not only had books fueled my interest in First World War aviation; like many of my fellow First World War aviation historians, while growing up I built dozens of model airplanes. One group of aircraft kits that were sold by Renewal were quite unique: instead of painting the model, you affixed an already decorated tissue that glued onto the aircraft.

This line of model airplanes really caught my attention, because these models "melded" the

pilot's story to his aircraft, since each kit had a brief biography of the pilot and discussed that pilot's unique markings. After several kits, you could mail in a coupon for a small poster of the pilots. Like all of those models, that poster which had hung on the wall in my bedroom above the carefully displayed model airplanes also went missing somehow and somewhere over the years.

However, my interest in the stories of the pioneering military pilots and the aircraft they flew

Above: An example of the personal markings to be found on many aircraft from WWI, in this case, an Italian Macchi N.11 fighter.

only grew over the years. And the desire to discover what the" imagery "of their world must have been for those early aviators , at least in my mind, changed from the appearance of model aircraft to becoming fascinated with aviation art.

That interest led to many contacts with aviation artists over the past years and I have always been amazed at the generosity of those artists. They, almost uniformly, not only helped to foster my interest in aviation art and with it the concept of visual history; the artists were very forthcoming in allowing me to utilize their works for this project. As I made contact with numerous artists from around the world, I learned that there was a prevailing sense of respect and an almost awe that the artists felt concerning their "subjects". The artwork created was often a labor of love, fueled by an avowed interest in the subject of First World War aviation within the artist.

Although I tried very hard and sometimes the process took several years, I was not always successful in "tracking down" an artist. One story in particular comes to mind. Sometime in early 2011, a good friend of mine notified me of a group of art prints for sale on ebay/Australia. These art prints were concerning a variety of first world war aviation

subjects and had apparently been found in a house that was undergoing renovation. I purchased the prints and then tried to identify the artist. Because of some outstanding help, via my friend Jim Dietz, I was able to identify the artist as a New Zealander: John N. Richards. But even now I have not yet successfully made contact with either him or any of his immediate family. Perhaps, someone reading this book can help me to establish contact: as i want to give full and due credit if possible. However I felt that his artwork, while being relatively unknown, was too good to be left out of this book and since I have not seen any examples of his work published elsewhere, I have used a few examples in order to recognize his talents.

His story is just one example of so many searches that I made over the many previous years, most of the time I have had the luck to be able to directly communicate with so many of the remarkable aviation artists whose work is to be found in these volumes.

Over the last nine years I have been fortunate enough to have had the privilege to work with Jack Herris and a group of outstanding aviation historians to produce a trilogy of aviation art books that told the stories of varied aspects of first world war

Above: Dogfight by New Zealand artist, John Richards.

aviation through text, photos and the superlative art of Steve Anderson, Jim Dietz and Russell Smith.

My goal in this book, ART OF THE DOGFIGHT, is to continue the concepts that I used in that trilogy of books. To bring alive as accurately as possible the history of First World War aviation by text, and photos in supplemental roles to the visual , "active", history that art can uniquely depict.

I began this project nearly twenty-five years ago! During those years I have been lucky enough to come to know aviation artists such as Brian Knight, Roy Cross, William Marsalko and many others. Sadly, some of these talented artists have gone west but I am very proud to be able to share their work in this volume.

This book's aim will be to cover the story of World War I aviation in a manner that has not yet been done outside of my other books and at the same time attempt to be more thorough than any other prior aviation art book that may have partially covered this subject matter.

For the First World War I aviation enthusiast that has already read and extensively studied this subject, there may not be too much new in the text of the stories. However I have tried my best to find new photos for most of the chapters and I have no doubt that the reader will find the artwork very interesting.

To the reader who may be interested in military history, or aviation history, or the study of the First World War but is not yet too familiar with the subject of military aviation in WWI: then I truly believe this compendium will be able to provide a solid start to the study of the many fascinating individuals, their aircraft and their exploits that combine to become the story of World War One aviation.

At the very least, my sincere hope is that these volumes will provide a very tangible way for those of us who are already enthusiastic historians of First World War aviation to share our field of study with the next generation of First World War aviation historians.

Jim Wilberg
Portland, Maine

18

Above: An evocative image of British SE5a fighters taking off on a "dawn patrol".

Left: A portrait of American pursuit pilot William Wellman, which can easily excite the imagination of a young boy as he dreams of taking to the skies in the First World War. George Evans

Before August 1914

Above: An evocative seen somewhere along the coast of France just before the outbreak of the First World War. Jim Dietz

"...the readiness to take to the air was a sign of national vitality and a reassuring indication that young people were willing to subject themselves to a demanding discipline and to give up their lives for the sake of higher values. By contrast, not to do so-to yield the air to one's adversaries-would be to demonstrate a dismaying lack of moral fiber and national determination."
Robert Wohl, *A Passion for Wings*
Yale University Press, 1994, p. 259

On 25th July 1909 Louis Bleroit flew across the English Channel in flight that took 35 minutes. From 22nd August until the 29th August 1909 the first official aviation meet was held outside Reims, France. There were contests of distance, altitude and speed. Of the 22 aviators who participated, only 2 were not French.

Since managing the first, controlled heavier-than-air flight, the Wright brothers and the majority of the nascent American aviation industry had taken a back seat to Europe and especially the French. Jules Vedrines was the first pilot to exceed 100 mph in 1912 and then flew from Paris to Cairo in 1913. Adolphe Pegoud had flown an aerobatic loop in September 1913 and had begun to thrill crowds by parachuting from his aircraft that same year.

And not only were the aviators making rapid strides, the capability of their machines was as well. The average speed for the winner of the Schneider Trophy race went from 45 mph in 1913 to over 86 mph the next year.

The public marveled at the newest heroes, these conquerors of the air. Their exploits were extensively covered and fantastical renditions of their flights could be found in the newspapers and journals of the day. The names of Vedrines, Pegoud, Garros and others were well-known not just in Europe but throughout the world.

And so the successes became a means of identifying who were the bravest, who were the most skilled and a means of tallying which culture produced the best aviators. It was before the war

Above: Maybe another day at the same aviation meet, or perhaps a different aviation meet, the crowds and their aviator heroes are there once again. Jim Dietz

that the term "ace" was used first. Many French periodicals had previously denoted champion sportsmen as les As, indicating that they were the "top of the deck". Therefore, the most successful aviators also become aces themselves: a term that would have its own, distinct measure of success in

Above: After his successful flight across the channel, Bleroit began to sell his monoplane throughout the world, here a Swiss Bleroit takes flight.

Above: RFC Bleroits photographed at Wantage during Army maneuvers in Sept, 1913.

Below: A Henri-Farman biplane similar to the ones used by H.F.19 in during their impressive feat.

PELLETIER D'OISY
Le Héros du raid Paris-Tokio

58

A.N.
PARIS

Left: Georges Pelletier D'Oisy during his service in WW I: he would survive the war and continue to make daring long-distance flights.

23

A French Navy Depredussion readies for a trail launch from a ship in 1913.

Aircraft are brought to the staring line for an air race at Hendon, England in 1913 - the aircraft "in flight" is likely montaged onto the photo; it is a Henri Farman biplane.

Above: Jules Vedrines readies his Borel floatplane in 1913.

the First World War.

It is likely that the risks faced by the aviators, the obvious perils to their safety only enhanced their hero status by the vast majority of people for whom flying an airplane was simply and thoroughly unbelievable. The number of crashes and deaths that the public read only magnified the status of those aviators who achieved the next record speed or altitude or distance.

In the years before the outbreak of war, the pace of of technological advances was nearly as impressive as the courage of the early aviators who took the ever changing aircraft designs and engines aloft. The understanding of aerodynamics was truly in its infancy.

All of the first aviators were essentially test pilots as they struggled to understand the parameters of powered flight.

And yet, in 1913 future fighter ace Georges Pelletier D'Oisy was a member of escadrille

H.F. 19 when it completed a 4,000 km mission circumnavigating France in which there were no crashes! The pace of advances in aviation in the few years leading up to the First World War was quite staggering. These advances are often overlooked as a modern reader views photographs of the apparently frail aircraft of the time.

Hence, it is in this arena that Jim DIetz's painting *BON TEMPS* must be viewed. A pre-war aviation meet on a European coast somewhere with throngs of people coming to see the bravest of the brave attempt to win a race or attempt new acrobatic maneuvers.

The moment in that painting is just a matter of a very short period of time before the "Guns of August" will roar and the aviators of the various nations will find themselves competing with each other in a new arena, more deadly than they could have ever imagined.

In the Beginning

Above: A German Taube as seen in flight.

Even though the field of aviation had taken comparatively big strides in terms of the capability in performance of the aircraft available at the time and there had already been some isolated, rather minuscule efforts regards exploration of military uses of the aircraft before August, 1914: in truth, the leaders of the various European military forces did not have any true sense of how their aviation units were best utilized. Other than a sense of reconnaissance capability and perhaps some

nuisance bombing role, the aviators were left to prove themselves and develop the worth of military aviation on their own, initially with very little oversight by the staff officers of the various armies.

It is therefore somewhat ironic, that a reasonable argument can be made that the biggest influences that aviation made in the First World War were made at the start of the war. It can also be argued that the nascent aviation units shaped how the remainder of the war would be fought before the military staffs

Left: How the Taube appeared to the Russian infantry it spied upon at Tannenberg. Alan Forbes

Facing Page, Above: Another view of a German Taube, critical to the German victory at Tannenberg. Russell Smith

Facing Page, Below: A modern Taube replica in flight shows the avian semblance of the aircraft.

Below Left: A contemporary sketch of the dangers facing German aviators on the Eastern Front.

had actually grasped the importance of aviation itself!

Consider the outcome of the three largest battles at the beginning of the war.

The Russian government had promised to invade German East Prussia as soon as possible at the outbreak of the war to force the Germans into splitting their forces to fight on two-fronts and thus sparing the French from the full weight of German military capability.

Therefore, the Russians dutifully marched a major force of approximately 600,000 men, divided into two armies of roughly equal size, into an offensive near the Masurian lakes region of East Prussia. The topography influenced the Russian strategy of splitting their forces into two independently functioning armies.

As the Russians advanced, the distance between the forces grew and the ability to communicate between them was hampered. The vast separation of the Russians was discovered by German aviators and promptly relayed to the German staff, which trusted the information. This allowed the German commander, Field Marshall von Hindenburg, to deal with the Russian forces separately without fear of being overwhelmed by superior numbers.

They call us "THE EYES OF THE ARMY"
For we scout for the foe far and wide,
And with all Information worth having
We keep the powers fully supplied –
There are Corps who bear much longer records
For brave deeds, yet History will find
That in the great fight
for the cause of the right,
OUR AIRMEN were not FAR BEHIND.

FROM ONE OF THE
R.F.C.

Above: A contemporary RFC postcard. Artist unknown.

Above: Aviation began to be utilized on all fronts, here is an Austrian Fokker B.II in the Mountains.

Right: A Morane-Saulnier takes off for a reconnaissance sortie early in the war.

Right: A Bleroit monoplane of the French AIr Service.

Right: A Bleroit in flight.

Left: A contemporary painting by William Lionel Wyllie(1915) depicts the clear advantage of aerial reconnaissance.

In a series of several battles the Germans decimated the Russians, which in a relatively quick timeframe effectively enfeebled the Russian military capability for the remainder of the war and thus allowed the German High Command to confidently focus its attention almost exclusively on the Western Front. Field Marshall von Hindenburg himself later wrote, "Without the airmen–no Tannenberg".

The German offensive on the Western front was both bold and ruthless as the German military swept through neutral Belgium on its way to attempt to separate the British Expeditionary Forces from the French Armies protecting Paris.Here again, the early

Above: The Royal Flying Corps had multiple types of aircraft at the start of the war, this is a Vickers pusher aircraft, which would eventually be mounted with a machine gun and would then be known as the Vickers Gunbus.

Above: A Royal Aircraft Factory B.e. 2 observation aircraft, which would become the mainstay of the RFC for far too long on the Western Front.

Above: An Albatros B.II aircraft is readied for a flight; note the aircrew reviewing their planned flightpath.

aviation units clearly played an important role in the outcome of two of the most significant battles of the first year of World War I.

This time it was the Allied air units who achieved considerable success despite their limited numbers and also, at least initially, skeptical army staff.

It would be good to remember at this point, that Louis Bleroit had first flown across the English Channel in 1909, using his type XI monoplane. Now, the first contingent of the Royal Flying Corps flew across the same channel on 13th August 1914; although this time there would be a total of 60 aircraft from numbers 2,3 and 4 squadrons. In almost exactly five years, what had been at first extraordinary had become almost routine. Lt. H.D. Harvey-Kelly of no.2 squadron would be the first to land at Amiens, France after a flight of one hour and fifty-five minutes (Bleroit's record setting flight had been just over thirty minutes).

On the 22nd of August, French forces began a complete re-deployment of their units from the right flank of the BEF (British Expeditionary Force), without informing the British commander and thus leaving the entire British force vulnerable to encirclement and destruction. It would be aviators who first informed the BEF command that the French had moved out of their positions on the right flank.It was a very perilous time for the British forces, but the fledgling RFC units (Royal Flying Corps) would put aircraft into the air on reconnaissance missions at least six to seven times a day.

The British aviators would prove to be invaluable in keeping track of the location of the advancing German forces and thus giving the British generals adequate time to fill gaps and prevent being flanked as the British forces retreated and regrouped. The British aviators also were able to quickly provide very accurate information about the location of the various British units as well, which allowed the retreat from the Mons River to never become a rout.

At first, the information was greeted with skepticism by the staff officers, but with repeated

Above: Another view of an Albatros B.II: note that the observer is in the front seat as he demonstrates the use of his camera.

Right: Ltn. Von Hiddessen, the pilot of the "5 o'clock Taube".

reports of critical information that seemed to be unerringly correct, the RFC airmen quickly were regarded as crucial to the success at saving the BEF. For example, on the 26th August 1914, a 2nd. Lt. Vivian Wadham was brought directly to his commander in chief, Sir John French, to give his report!

The RFC airman would often take off from one location, land near a divisional headquarters to report, and be told to then land at a new "airfield" since the retreat was so fast, that the ground was being constantly ceded to the Germans, in order to save the BEF itself. The successful retreat and eventual re-alignment with the French forces denied the efforts of the German First Army to envelop the British forces and thus kept Britain in the war.

Sir John French later wrote about the RFC following the Battle of the Mons: "Fired at constantly by both friend and foe, and not hesitating to fly in every kind of weather, they have remained undaunted throughout...They have furnished me with the most complete and accurate information

Above: A German Albatros B.II engages a RFC Be2 in a rare encounter in the early days of the war. Steve Anderson

which has been of incalculable value in the conduct of the operations."

Louis Breguet was a very famous pre-war aviator and one of the pre-eminent aircraft designers in France. At the outbreak of the war, he flew his own personal aircraft to a French military airfield and offered both himself and his aircraft in service to his country.

The German forces were forced to adjust their plans of attack following the successful retreat of the BEF and so the Germans now began to swing further southeast than originally planned. Breguet spotted a large gap between the two shifting German armies on the 2nd of September, 1914. At first his information was dismissed, however several other French aviators reported similar observations and finally the chief aviation officer for the French Sixth Army, Captain Bellinger, refused to continue to ignore these reports and on his own initiative brought them to the attention of General Joseph-

Simon Gallieni, who was the commander of the French forces defending Paris.

Acting on these reports, Gallieni initiated the counterattack on the 6th September that became known as the Battle of the Marne. This successful attack caused the Germans to end their autumn offensive and even retreat to more favorable locations in order to build a strong trench system of defense from further Allied offensive actions: initiating the rapid construction of the opposing trench systems that would eventually stretch from the English Channel to Switzerland.

Hence, military aviation rapidly went from an uncertain "add-on" to a fully recognized and invaluable element of reconnaissance: the reports of aviators engaged in reconnaissance would be considered essential knowledge for any actions contemplated by the commanding officers at all levels of the army.

It seems that the German aviators on the

Above: A contemporary color photo of a Caudron in the French Air Service.

Western Front did not have similar results to their counterparts during the Battle of Tannenberg. However, Ltn. Ferdinand von Hiddessen made a remarkable flight on the 30th August when he flew his Taube over Paris. He and his observer dropped four bombs and dropped numerous copies of a message that read:

"The German Army is at the Gates of Paris. There is nothing for you to do but surrender.

Lt. Von Hiddessen"

His mission took 2.5 hours from his aerodrome at Saint-Quentin in Northern France. Indeed, the German forces were a mere 30 miles away from Paris at the time. He would return on several occasions over the next few days, along with some other German aviators in their aircraft. The French published his message in the daily newspapers and began to scan the skies above Paris in the late afternoon to see the German intruders. The intended

desire of inciting panic in the population did not occur and soon enough the German aviators were given other missions once the Battle of the Marne commenced.

Lt. Von Hiddessen himself would be seriously wounded, shot down and captured during the Battle of Verdun. He would recover from his wounds and survive the war.

The early military aviators and their relatively few number of aircraft that could be seen in the skies over the front lines and boldly venturing behind the battlefronts as well in the autumn of 1914, crucially shaped the outcome of the First World War's first major actions to such a degree that going forward, there would be calls again and again by all military staffs for more aviators and more aircraft with the result that aviation would be considered as instrumental from that point onwards to the conduct of the combatants in the war.

Above: The so-called "5 o'clock Taube" over Paris. Merv Corning

Growing Talons

Above: A fine study of Avro 789, which would have been the same as 398.

As soon as the military staff of the various belligerent nations realized how accurate and valuable the reconnaissance from their air assets could be, an emphasis was placed on rapidly growing the number of available aircraft and for improving the designs of the aircraft to improve the capability of "seeing beyond the horizon".

And as quickly, the aviators involved took it upon themselves to deny the enemy while protecting their own reconnaissance aircraft. Thus, from almost the very start of the First World War, combat ascended into the heavens.

There were at first, no specifically designed fighter aircraft and the ability to arm the aircraft had also yet to be designed. Therefore, the more aggressive of the aviators took rifles, side arms and a variety of other weapons aloft with which to attack their counterparts.

The very first recognized aerial victory should be credited to the Royal Flying Corps for the action that took place on 25th August 1914. That afternoon Lt. C.W. Wilson and Lt. C.E.C. Rabagliati of Number 5 Squadron were at their airfield, while their Avro 504 aircraft was being re-fuelled following an earlier reconnaissance flight.

A German Taube was seen coming towards their airfield, whereupon the commanding officer of 5 Sqdn., Major J.F.A."Josh" Higgins, shouted at the two aviators to "go and take his number!". The two took off and while Wilson piloted their aircraft to be in front and slightly below the German aircraft, Rabagliati fired away with his rifle which was aimed backwards over Wilson's head since the observer, Rabagliati, was in the front seat of the Avro. Later Rabagliati stated that the two aircraft circled each other for "some time" and that he had fired 100 rounds from his rifle in the engagement.

They saw the German descend into a forced landing, however the British crew was not exactly certain where they were in regards to the ground forces and so the two British aviators returned to their airfield near Le Cateau. Upon landing, they discovered that the German had actually force landed quite close by and so the two drove out to claim their prize.

Arriving at the German Taube, they discovered Lt. Harvey-Kelly posing beside the aircraft as the victor! Lt. H.D. Harvey-Kelly and his observer Lt.

Above: A photo of Harvey-Kelly lying down and enjoying a cigarette next to his BE2a, after a forced landing somewhere in France, he initially believed he had scored the RFC's first air-to-air victory.

W.H.C. Mansfield of No.2 Sqdn. in their B.E. 2a aircraft had apparently engaged the same aircraft as it was descending to land, firing at it with their revolvers. Kelly had landed beside the aircraft and the two of them had chased the German crew into a nearly woods.

Below: Photo 2a: A modern replica BE2 of Harvey-Kelly's machine.

Above: Wilson and Robagliati in Avro 398 score the Royal Flying Corps first victory. Peter Dennis

Right: The early aviators began to arm their aircraft in anyway that made sense, here a Nieuport 10 has had a machine gun mounting to fire over the propeller arc fixed for the observer to use. Rene Prejelan

Above: Piotor Nesterov beside his Nieuport monoplane.

Above: A contemporary color photo of a Morane Sualnier L, known to everyone as the Parasol.

Above: A formal portrait of Nesterov.

"He [Harvey-Kelly] had landed beside it and he and his observer had chased the pilot into a wood. They had removed a small plaque from the wreckage, which they were now displaying as booty, 'Stopped him in full career,' wrote Wilson in his diary,'and claimed first Hun for 398[the identification number of their Avro]. H-K handed the plaque gracefully to me, "Your bird I think."' WIlson and Rabagliati passed the trophy on to Higgins laconically,'"Number you asked for, Sir."" [Barker, *THE RFC IN FRANCE*,p.39]

Chronologically at least, the next victory in air combat came at a steep price. Piotr Nesterov was a superb, pre-war pilot who likely completed the first successful loop in September of 1913. He was assigned to the Russian XI Air Corps as its commander at the outbreak of the war and Nesterov was the kind of pilot that wanted to attack the

Above: Georges Guynemer demonstrates his machine gun and its mounting device on his Morane-Saulnier Parasol aircraft, similar in some regards to the machine gun mounting as depicted in the sketch by Prejelan.

Left: Frantz (pilot) on the left and Quenault (observer/gunner) on the right beside the tail of their Voison aircraft after having been awarded medals for their aerial victory.

enemy, despite not having much in the way of a useful weapon to accomplish the task.

Nesterov's command was based near the town of Zholkov, it had been less than a year following his successful acrobatics. On 7th September, 1914 the aerodrome was attacked by an Austro-Hungarian Lohner aircraft which dropped several small bombs. Nesterov was incensed at this unanswered provocation! The next day, the Austro-Hungarian aircraft (the Lohner was commanded by its observer Oblt. Friedrich Rosenthal, its pilot was Feldwebel Franz Malina) returned early in the morning and again proceeded to bomb the airfield. This time Nesterov was prepared, mounting into his Morane-Saulnier type G fighter and proceeded to attack the enemy aircraft, armed with only a pistol.

HIs attacks proved less than ideal, and the unworried Austro-Hungarian crew returned yet again at mid-day to bomb the airfield and once again Nesterov attempted to down the enemy via his pistol fire without any success.

When the Austro-Hungarians attacked for the third time on the same day, it proved too much of a personal insult to Nesterov. This time, instead of firing his pistol, Nesterov flew above his enemy and then dove upon the unsuspecting Lohner aircraft and deliberately rammed it. The unsurprising results were that both the Russian and the Austro-Hungarians crashed to their deaths.

The first air-to-air combat victory may well have been in late September, 1914 when German naval aviator Gunther Plushow claimed to have shot down a Japanese Maurice Farman utilizing his parabellum mauser pistol (for details please see the chapter Dragon Master of Tsingtao).

The first undisputed air-to-air combat victory went to a French crew of *escadrille* V. 24. Throughout the First World War, the French Air Force would identify their units by the type of aircraft they were flying, therefore in this case *escadrille* 24 was flying the Voison 3LA two-seat aircraft. The advantage this aircraft had was that it was a "pusher" aircraft, the engine was behind the aircrew, who sat in a "bathtub" style fuselage.

The aircraft was able to mount a light weight 8mm Hotchkiss machine gun that was mounted to fire forward and manned by the observer who sat behind the pilot. This allowed the pilot to concentrate on flying the aircraft and also allowed the pilot to assist his observer/gunner by simply flying straight at the enemy aircraft in order to give a good field of fire.

Most of the two seat aircraft of the day had the observer in the front cockpit which necessitated the pilot to fly alongside the other aircraft in order to allow for a shot by the observer.

Thus, on 5th October 1914 Sgt. Joseph Frantz (pilot) and Sapeur Louis Quenault (observer/gunner) shot down an Aviatik B.I from *Feldflieger Abteilung* 18 for the first, confirmed air to air victory. It was not an easy task as Quenault fired two 48-round magazines from his Hotchkiss machine gun(firing one round at a time as the gun was prone to jam) and still the Aviatik flew on. Quenault then took out a carbine and after several shots, wounded the pilot and forced the Germans to crash near Reims(both German aviators were killed).

The news of the aerial victory quickly spread throughout the French AIr Force and inspired some of the more courageous and intrepid pilots to innovate variations on weapons and begin to develop the tactics of air combat (see chapter *Les As*).

Another early, innovative fighter pilot would be found on the Eastern Front. At the outbreak of the war Alexander Kozakov was flying a Morane-Saulnier G monoplane in Poland with the IV Corps Air Detachment. He devised a method of dangling a

Above: Kozakov in his Morane-Saulnier aircraft, note the Imperial Russian double eagle on the cowling.

Below: A formal portrait of Kozakov.

stout wire with an anchor below his aircraft, within the anchor was an explosive charge that Kozakov could activate from his cockpit once the anchor had entangled itself into the enemy's aircraft.

On the 31st March 1915 Kozakov had his chance and used his device to attack a German Albatros reconnaissance aircraft. However, the anchor went past the German aircraft and the wire became entangled in the enemy aircraft which prevented Kozakov from activating his plan. Kozakov then decided to ram the enemy's top wing with his

Above: A view of what was to come, a Sopwith Gordon Bennett racer now fitted with a Lewis machine gun and metal deflectors on the propeller.

Above: A group of Russian pilots, perhaps talking about the best way to attack their enemy in the sky: note the unarmed Morane-Saulnier monoplanes.

Left: The first true air-to-air victory by Frantz and Quenault. Merv Corning

Above: Kozakov scoring his first victory, although his trailing anchor device did not actually perform as expected and in the end, he was forced to actually ram his victim. Merv Corning

undercarriage (another example of a Russian deliberately ramming an enemy).

Unfortunately, the tail of Kozakov's Morane became caught in the German's wingtip and the two aircraft began plummeting towards earth. Only a few hundred feet from a fatal crash, Kozakov's aircraft became free and he managed a controlled crash landing without any injury and only minor damage

to his aircraft.

However, as a means of trying to obtain air supremacy, ramming your opponent was not likely to be very successful and as costly to you as to the enemy! Air warriors needed to develop more reliable weapons and effective means of using them before they could truly envision their birds of prey as having useful talons.

Les As

Above: Garros in his floatplane before the war.

It seems that most aviation historians have not seen fit to give appropriate kudos to the courageous and innovative French aviators who, in 1914 and 1915, first developed the means with which to consistently and effectively attack their enemy's aircraft and thus were able to claim air superiority over the battlefield.

Well before there was a Fokker scourge, there were skilled French aviators aggressively using their aircraft, principally the Morane-Saulnier L at first, to try to clear the skies of German aircraft. How many readers of aviation history are aware of Roland Garros and his ingenious deflector blades. And it is likely that there are even fewer readers who are aware that before Garros there was Eugene Gilbert, who along with other French pilots such as Pegoud, Navarre, Guynemer, Vedrines and Nungesser took command of the skies over their sections of the Western Front.

Before the war, French newspapers and periodicals began referring to winning auto racers or bike racers or any number of sports heroes as "Les As"- an implication to the ace as the top card of any suit. Once the war began, the weekly periodicals began to refer to aviators who downed an enemy plane in similar fashion and therefore the term "ace" came into the vernacular.

Eventually, it became customary to ascribe the title of ace to an aviator who had at least five confirmed victories, although the Germans had their own "rules": they would utilize the term "Kanone" and it would take ten confirmed victories to earn that title.

However, in the early winter of 1914 there were not that many aircraft in the air and it could be many days before a front line combat pilot even saw

Garros, far right, managed to be flamboyant and dress well even in captivity.

48

Above: Eugene Gilbert actually began his "training" in aerial combat before the war began. While attempting a flight over the Pyrenees Mountains in 1911 he was attacked by an irate eagle which he fended off with several shots from a revolver.

Facing Page, Below: Arguably the world's first dedicated fighter squadron, M.S.12 in 1915, these men began the concept of specialized fighter pilots: form left to right and utilizing the numbers on the photograph: 5.Lt. Paul Gastin, 2. Capt. Auguste Le Reverend, 6. Adj. Georges Pelletier d"Oisy, 1.Capt. Charles Tricoronot de Rose(chief of aviation for the 5th Army), 7. Adj.Pierre Clement, 3.Lt. Raymond de Bernis(commander M.S.12), 8. sLt. Ferrer(obs), 9. Lt. Rene Chambe(obs), 10. Sgt.Jean Navarre, 11. Sgt. Rene Mesguich, 12. Lt. Robert Jacottet(obs), 4. Lt. Gabriel Pelege(obs), 13. Lt.Jean Moinier(obs)– all are pilots except the observers as noted.

Above: Pegoud, on the left, in front of his Nieuport fighter, he may have been the world's first official fighter ace- however he has two claimed victories that have remained only "semi-official".

Left: In the beginning, the French aircrews of M.S.12 and other units had to make do with attacking German opponents with carbines, revolvers, and occasionally a light machine gun.

an enemy aircraft, much less have the opportunity to engage it in combat. Therefore each early dogfight was significant and much was written about these early "aces" and many conversations were had, regarding the earliest *chasse* (hunter) pilots who would be the forerunners of fighter pilots.

Several of the most famous pre-war French aviators took it upon themselves to pioneer the art of fighter aviation. At first, the most successful pilot was Eugene GIlbert who had raced motorcycles before becoming involved with racing aircraft before the start of the war. At the start of the war Gilbert found himself in *escadrille M.S. 23* along with other

notable aviators such as Marc Pourpe and Roland Garros. Fortunately for Gilbert, their aircraft was one of the fastest and most maneuverable types in the French Air Force at the time: the Morane-Saulnier Type L, usually known as the Parasol because of the location of the wing reminded people of a parasol.

At this time, the Parasol was used as a two-seater observation aircraft and also used on what was known as "special missions", in which spies were landed or retrieved from behind enemy lines. However, pilots such as Gilbert were not going to allow the speed and the agility of their

Above: Eugene Gilbert – a case can be made that he became the world's first official fighter ace, the first to score five victories. The official record of the French Air Service in WWI credits Georges Guynemer as its first official ace by scoring his fifth official victory on 3rd February 1915.

Above: Gilbert beside his M.S. N fighter, which may actually have been the first of its design ever built: it was intended as a racer that Roland Garros was to fly before the start of the war.

Above: Roland Garros scored his first victory with his new invention on 1st April 1915. Seweryn Fleischer
Below: Gilbert in flight in his "Le Vengeur": A clear indication that he was intent on avenging the loss of his friend Garros.

Adolf Pegoud

La Grande Guerre 1914-1915.
Visé Paris 387

Roland Garros

LE SOUS-LIEUTENANT GARROS

Jean Navarre

LE SOUS-LIEUTENANT NAVARRE

Eugene Gilbert

LE SOUS-LIEUTENANT GILBERT

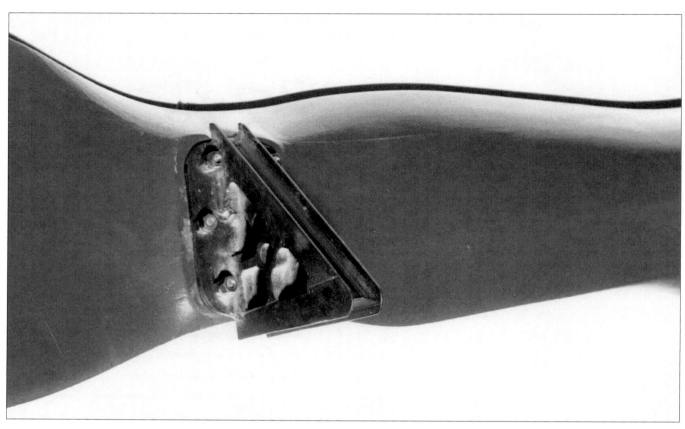

Above: An example in the collection of the NASM of the deflector blades used by the French and then other Allied aircraft that had been fabricated by Garros and his mechanic.

Below: Another of the famous pre-war French pilots, Jules Vedrines, beside his M.S. N fighter as he prepares for a mission.

Above: Vedrines displays his well-recognized sang froid by continuing to smoke his cigarette while in the cockpit, despite the proximity of his gasoline tank and ammunition.

Above: An unidentified French pilot in his M.S. N fighter, the aircraft was reputed to be difficult to fly but with the mounted machine gun, in the hands of a talented pilot, could wreak havoc upon their German foes.

Above: The single seat Morane-Saulnier N would find service in nearly every Allied air service, here is an example of a Russian fighter, now equipped with a Vickers machine gun that is synchronized to fire through the propeller blade. Tony Theobold

Above: The M.S. N fighter found its way into almost all of the Allied air services, this image shows a RFC "Bullet" about to take off, note the ground crew holding onto the aircraft as the engine is revved to gain enough speed.

Above: The commander of all aviation units for the French 5th Army, de Rose is given credit for organizing his units into escadrilles of singular purpose and thus created the first chasse or fighter squadrons in order to maximize their efficiency and gain air superiority in the skies above the Verdun battlefield.

Right: A Nieuport 11 fighter over the trenches, with the introduction of the nimble and fast Nieuport "Babe" fighter, the French began to be increasingly successful against their German opponents.

Above: French ace. Lt. Armand de Turenne of esc. N.48 and a comrade patrol the skies over Verdun in their Nieuport 11 fighters. The French fighter pilots were able to gain command because of this aircraft and their happiness in their success, combined with their patriotism of protecting such a symbolic place as Verdun, lead to colorful displays of the blue-white-red of the national flag, de Turenne also displays his family's coat of arms in a hunting horn. Seweryn Fleischer

The Nieuport 11 was in effect, a downsized version of earlier Nieuport fighters (hence the Bebe nickname): shown here is a Nieuport 10 fighter which was created by eliminating the space for an observer, and mounting a machine gun on to the top wing.

Above: For several weeks Roland Garros struck fear in the German aviation units opposite of him, several other French pilots followed in his footsteps as they modified their Parasol scouts with a forward firing machine gun. Taras Shytk

aircraft to go to waste. On 2nd November 1914 he engaged a German Taube with the commander of M.S. 23, Capt. Maire de Lomotte as his observer. Lomotte fired 30 rounds from his carbine and forced the German to crash. Relatively quickly, on 18 November GIlbert scored again as he and his observer, Auguste Bayle, engaged with a German LVG B.I and forced it to land behind French lines.

Then on 10 January 1915 Gilbert maneuvered his Parasol into a position that allowed his observer, Lt. Alphonse de Puechredon to fire several times at a German Rumpler B.I. His first shots wounded the pilot, Lt. Franz Keller and after several more shots, de Puechredon had killed the German observer and damaged the radiator forcing Lt. Keller to land behind French lines near Villers-Bocage. The French

aviators landed nearby to claim their prize, but upon finding the wounded Keller, they made efforts to help him until medical personnel could arrive. Upon hearing that his victor was the famous pre-war pilot Eugene Gilbert, Keller forced himself onto his feet in order to shake Gilbert's hand out of respect for the skilled aviator. Gilbert would fly over the lines the next day in order to drop several messages and a letter that Keller had written to his mother.

With these successes, Capt. Raymond Joseph de Bernis and Commander Charles Baron Tricornot, the Marquis de Rose worked together to convince the appropriate authorities that a specialized *escadrille de chasse* should be formed in order to clear the skies of German aircraft. Thus *escadrille* M.S. 12 was formed and trained into a true fighter squadron

Left: With the growing number of successes, a new hero was born, the fighter ace: the public would eagerly read stories of the thrills of flying and the dangers, the excitement of air combat: stories that the propaganda services were quick to utilize to their purposes. Rene Prejelan

Below: With the intense air battles over Verdun, and with the advent of the improved fighter aircraft, a new generation of French aces emerged, here is Sgt. Henri Barnay who landed next to his second confirmed victory, a German Rumpler C.I that he forced to land behind French lines on 19 May 1916. Barnay himself would not join the growing ranks of French aces, he would have no further success in air combat and be posted out of the Air Service!

Above: Capt. De Rose would fly his Nieuport 11 in combat so as to best understand if his strategy was effective and to help him understand the tactics his pilots were employing. Tragically, de Rose would die in a crash while demonstrating his aircraft to the French staff of the 5th Army. Andrew Dillon

utilizing the speedy Parasol and the two chose their unit's aviators based on a sense of keenness to engage the enemy(the initial aircraft of the unit had been the Nieuport VI two-seater which had been used for reconnaissance).

After some training on the new aircraft in February, the unit was sent to the front lines on 1 March 1915 with the sole purpose of attacking and downing enemy aircraft: the first true fighter squadron of all time.

At this same time, another unit, *escadrille* M.S. 37 was also formed as a *chasse* or fighter squadron. Gilbert would transfer to M.S. 37 where he would join Adolphe Pegoud, who along with Garros may have been among the most famous of all the French pre-war aviators. Pegoud had been a test pilot for the Bleriot aviation company and had a world-renowned name. Pegoud had begun the war with M.F. 25 flying slow, cumbersome observation aircraft and he was not going to miss out on his chance to join in on sweeping the *Boche* from the skies!

Pegoud modified things by attaching a Hotchkiss machine gun to his aircraft so that his gunner, his friend and aircraft mechanic from before the war, Leon Lerendu, could pepper the enemy much more effectively than using only a carbine. On 5 February, Pegoud and Lerendu may have forced down three German aircraft in a single day! They then forced a German Taube to land behind French lines on 2 April. And on the 28th April the two downed an Aviatik, with the result that Pegoud is likely able to claim the title of first fighter pilot ace in history.

Hence, the French were now forming specific fighter squadrons and the aviators within them were aggressively attacking their enemy with demonstrable results.

However Roland Garros was not content. He reasoned that the most effective fighter would be a single seat aircraft in which the pilot could point his aircraft at the enemy and fire his weapon while flying directly at his target and not have to fly around the German in order to give his gunner an

Above: One of the actual Nieuport 11 aircraft that de Rose flew in the First World War has been restored and hangs in a museum in France, note his personal insignia.

angle to fire.

He devised a scheme (along with mechanic Jules Hue) where steel deflectors were placed on the propeller blade. He mounted a Hotchkiss machine gun on the fuselage immediately in front of the cockpit, so that now the pilot needed to only aim his aircraft at his enemy and he was thus simultaneously aiming his weapon as well. When fired, most of the bullets would miss the whirling propeller blades and the few that struck the blade would be deflected away(hopefully not to hit some vital portion of the aircraft). This scheme was aided by the fact that the French bullets were of copper, and so the steel deflectors themselves would not be damaged and would cause the bullets to shatter on impact. Garros managed to wrangle a transfer to M.S. 23 to be with his friend GIlbert and work on proving the worth of his device honing his fighter tactics with his friend.

On the 1st April 1915, Garros flew straight at a German biplane and it would be safe to assume the Germans felt safe in that Garros was not orbiting their aircraft in order to give his gunner a chance to fire. In fact, maybe the German's noted that Garros was alone in his Morane-Saulnier Parasol. In any case, Garros flew upon them and fired his machine gun through his own propeller blades and the German went down in flames. Garros would score two more times before being forced to land behind German lines by ground fire while on a bombing mission.

The Germans would study Garros's deflector blades and would give the aircraft over to Anthony Fokker to emulate the system devised by Garros for them (please refer to the chapter on Fokker for more details).

Another French aviator had scored a victory on 1st April, although still utilizing a gunner with a carbine. He was not a famous pre-war aviator like Garros or GIlbert but would become one of the most famous of the early French fighter pilots of the war: Jean Navarre, who was a pilot in M.S. 12(for more details on Navarre, please refer to chapter Sentinel of Verdun).

On 1st April, Navarre managed to slide his Parasol next to a German Aviatik and his gunner sLt. Robert fired three shots from his carbine- wounding both German aviators and forcing them to land behind French lines. Navarre would score again, on the 13th of April.

Now that the French had a means to fire through the propellor, the need for a gunner was gone and so what was needed was a small, fast, agile single seat fighter.

It was now that the Morane-Saulnier N type found itself on the front lines. In fact it was Gilbert who brought the first of its kind to the front lines when he transferred from M.S. 37 along with Adolphe Pegoud to a newly formed fighter *escadrille* M.S. 49. Here Gilbert was assigned the first type of the Morane-Saulnier fighter, likely the very aircraft that Garros had flown before the war in pre-war races and which now had deflector plates in place on the propeller. GIlbert named his aircraft *Le Vengeur* and went after the Germans to repay them for the loss of Garros. However, like his friend, Gilbert would be forced down on a bombing mission, he landed in Switzerland while flying back from a raid on the Zeppelin base in Friedrichshafen and was interred for much of the remainder of the war.

Meanwhile, the seemingly invincible Pegoud was killed in combat on 31 August 1915 by a German gunner in a two-place Aviatik that was being flown by a pre-war student pilot of Pegouds.

Pegoud and Pourpe killed, GIlbert and Garros captured: the ranks of the earliest French fighter pilots were starting to thin. However, there were still plenty of pilots with the needed *elan* to carry forth: pilots such as Navarre, Guynemer, Nungesser and Vedrines.

The French also had leaders in the ranks of the aviation commanders that had enough vision to continue to develop strategy and tactics for the future.

The Germans launched an offensive at Verdun with the hopes of "bleeding the French white". It was here that the commander of all aviation units attached to the 5th army, Commander de Rose established *group de combat* units. These units were composed of typically four *escadrilles* and each group was specialized into fighter, bombing or reconnaissance types. At this time, both the Germans and the British had one or two fighters assigned to squadrons which were also performing a mixed "bag" of mission types.

After combining his *escadrille de chasse* into one cohesive group, de Rose further increased their capabilities by giving them the freedom to determine how best to tactically achieve their goal, which he defined quite simply with an operational order that stated: "..seek the enemy in order to engage and destroy him".

The French were successful at securing air superiority during the battle of Verdun, in large measure because of their ability and willingness to recognize the importance of their air assets and the willingness to evolve in their deployment and the tactics those units would employ.

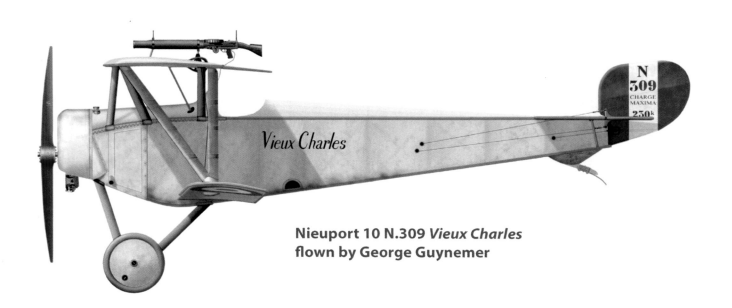

Nieuport 10 N.309 *Vieux Charles* flown by George Guynemer

Fokker Scourge

Left: The interrupter gear clearly shown, this Fokker variant was likely being developed before the capture of the French ace Roland Garros's aircraft.

Although the French chasse pilots would begin the battle for air supremacy by attacking their German counterparts with clear elan and unbridled vigor: their Hotchkiss machine guns, which required to be re-loaded after only 24 bullets in a clip and were prone to jamming quite often, as well as the limitations and inherent dangers of their deflector devices would clearly inhibit their overall success.

Therefore, the battlefield above the trenches on the Western Front would initially see its first viable and specific fighter aircraft in the summer of 1915. It was then that Anthony Fokker, a Dutch pre-war flyer and aircraft designer, would modify one of his existing designs, the result would be known as the Fokker E.I, the Fokker Eindecker (single wing, i.e. monoplane) fighter aircraft.

Roland Garros had been involved in a bombing mission behind German lines on 18 April 1915 , when his aircraft was damaged and he was forced to land. Garros set his aircraft on fire, however after the Germans had captured Garros and were able to inspect his aircraft, the deflector blades on the propellor could still be clearly examined. Thus, the German command wanted their own "device" quickly installed and utilized in a suitable aircraft in order to battle back against the aggressive actions of the French fighter pilots.

Fokker would do much better than simply copy the deflector mechanism of Garros- he would install his stangensteuerung (synchronizer mechanism) into one of his Fokker M5L (lange,long wing) monoplanes and develop what was essentially a flying gun.

Interestingly, Franz Schneider, a Swiss engineer, who had worked at Nieuport and then L.V.G. before the war had established a patent for a synchronization mechanism to fire a machine gun through the propellor of an airplane in July 1913. In fact, the details of his design were actually published in Flugsport journal in September, 1914.

No doubt incorporating some of these ideas in his process, an engineer working for Fokker, Heinrich Lubbe, had already been working on making a useful interrupter gear for a couple months before Garros was captured. A connecting rod was attached to the oil pump drive located on the rear of the rotary engine such that when a propellor blade would be in front of the gun, the connecting rod would interrupt the trigger and not allow the gun to fire.

Anthony Fokker, a very accomplished and talented pilot himself, flew his armed and modified M5L, now known as a Fokker E.I, in demonstration flights for the German authorities. He would fire at aircraft wings mounted on the ground and riddle them with bullets without any apparent damage his

Above: Boelcke aloft somewhere over Verdun in his Fokker E IV. Martinicky, courtesy of Eduard models.

Above: A photo showing Anthony Fokker in the cockpit of an M5L aircraft with the addition of a machine gun, in this case a Parabellum, note the headrest for the pilot. This could be the aircraft that Fokker flew to demonstrate his interrupter gear.

Above: The newly named Fokker E.I at the frontline. Fokker has his back to the camera with his cap on and is talking to the German Crown Prince: note the lack of national markings on the wings.

Above: Fokker (L) and Kurt Wintgens, Wintgens would score the first official victory in the new Fokker fighter, he had learned to fly at the Fokker-Schwerin facility and seemed to have become friends with the young Dutchman.

own aircraft propellor.

According to Fokker, he brought his machine to the airfield near Douai where FFA 62 was based. Fokker wrote that he himself was instructed to shoot down an enemy aircraft to prove the mission capability of his design. Fokker would write that during a flight, he snuck up on an unsuspecting French aircraft but could not pull the trigger. Apparently, it would be acceptable for Fokker the businessman to sell aircraft to the Germans during the war, but it would not be okay for Anthony Fokker the neutral Dutch citizen to actually participate in the shooting and killing.

During the course of the First World War, Anthony Fokker would become renowned for his marketing skills, although some of his stories would sometimes be called into question regards their authenticity. It is therefore not certain that Fokker actually flew over the front lines or not(see chapter, Flying Dutchman).

German aviators were not hampered by any such reluctance and two of the notable pilots who early on would demonstrate the effectiveness of the Fokker E.I to other pilots were Otto Parschau and Kurt Wintgens. In fact, Wintgens had learned to fly at the very start of the war at Fokker's factory located at Schwerin.

Likely at least because of his connections to Fokker, Wintgens was given one of the first Fokker E.I aircraft, 5/15 and sent to a part of the front where the opposing French pilots in their Morane-Saulnier Parasol L aircraft were making their "presence felt"[this statement was likely referring to Gilbert

Above: A Fokker Jagdflieger executes a classic zoom and re-attack maneuver that would become known as an Immelmann turn as he prepares for a second attack on a RFC BE2 observation aircraft. John Richards

Above: At first, the Fokker aircraft were sent to established FFA units (two-seat army co-operation) and were flown on "extra" sorties by selected pilots.

Above: A good look at an early Fokker fighter in flight.

and Pegoud who were active in this area].

On 2 July 1915, Wintgens shot down a French M-S L type from escadrille M.S. 48 wounding both the pilot Capt. du Peuty and the observer/gunner sLt. de Boutiny as well as damaging their engine. Because the French crew were able to land safely behind their lines, Wintgens was not given official confirmation for the victory although it is now recognized by historians as the first victory in what would become known as the Fokker Scourge.

This first victory already pointed to what would be the ultimate advantage the Fokker pilots would have: their synchronized, belt-fed machine gun which had a capacity of 500 bullets.

Wintgens managed to hit the French aircraft nearly 200 times before the crew was forced down. Neither the British or the French had any firepower of that capability in their aircraft.

The Fokker E series aircraft would prove to be of average or less than average flying characteristics,

Below: Ltn. Kurt Student, a Fokker ace, takes off: note the simple grass airfield.

Above: Eduard Bohme helps to load his Fokker's gun, one of the biggest advantages that the Fokker pilots had was the fact that they had a total of 500 rounds to use in their missions, allowing them to make repeated firing passes, which meant they could press their attacks until successful despite the very challenging art of deflection shooting required in combat.

Above: Fokkers fly past an observation balloon on their way to gain altitude and a position to patrol the front lines. Steve Anderson

but the difference was in the weapon the Fokker aircraft wielded.

Meanwhile, Lt, Parschau was demonstrating his Fokker E.I, 1/15, to the airmen of FFA 62 where Anthony Fokker had flown as well. Among the interested pilots were Lt. Max Immelmann and Lt. Oswald Boelcke. Both pilots had shown keenness in attacking the enemy while flying their reconnaissance sorties and therefore both were assigned to fly the Fokker monoplanes when possible.

At this time, both were still assigned their usual duties of flying the two-seater reconnaissance aircraft on the routine missions assigned to FFA 62. They were allowed, in fact they were encouraged, to fly additional missions in order to seek out the enemy in their new fighter aircraft.

For the summer of 1915 and for much of the

autumn of 1915, Fokker E. types would be sent in small numbers of 1-2 or 3 to each of the frontline FFA and in each case, the squadron commander would choose one or two pilots within his squadron to fly these aircraft on their new interceptor missions.

This would lead to an overall dilution of their effectiveness, however the effect of the new German fighter aircraft was still quickly felt. On 1 August 1915, BE 2 aircraft flew a mission to bomb the airfield of FFA 62 at Douai. In order to carry their small bombs, many of the aircraft had to leave the observers behind and so the British pilots were left on their own to fly the aircraft, deliver the payload on target and defend themselves with automatic pistols.

Both Boelcke and Immelmann responded to this intrusion and attacked the British squadron in their

Above: Eventually the Fokker monoplane fighters found their way to every front that Germany was involved in the fighting, here a pilot brings his Fokker in for a landing on the Eastern Front, one can only imagine how cold the pilot must be at this point in his mission.
Below: One of the earliest and most successful Fokker aces, Ltn. Max Mulzer prepares for a mission.

Above: Mulzer would become the first Bavarian airmen to receive the PLM and the fifth airman so honored. He would often fly with Immelmann at FFA 62 and was called Bavarian Max to differentiate from Saxon Max. His tunic was a green color, from his cavalry regiment which earned him the nickname "der Monsieur Grun" from the local female population as Mulzer was tall and apparently quite handsome. He would die in a fatal crash in September 1916.

Above: A Fokker being flown by Mulzer in escort to a two-seater Roland C.I. Review of records show that the overall loss of Allied aircraft during the Fokker Scourge was also in large part because of the offensive spirit and successes of the two-seater crews as well.

new Fokker monoplanes. It has been reported that the direct line of attack taken by the German pilots surprised the British aviators, since they had no knowledge of the new weapon capability.

Boelcke was the first to attack, but his machine gun jammed and he was compelled to fly off to attempt a clearing of his gun. Immelmann's gun worked perfectly and after firing off 450 rounds, Immelmann forced his opponent down. 2Lt. William Reid had been one of the BE2 aircraft without an observer/gunner and was not able to put up much of a fight. Amongst the numerous bullets Immelmann had let loose upon his opponent, two wounded Reid"s left arm and more bullets had punctured his fuel tank which necessitated his forced landing behind German lines. Immelmann landed next to his victim, and helped arrange expeditious medical care for Reid.Later that same day, Immelmann flew over the trenches to drop a message to the British forces to inform them of Reid's capture.

Thus began the mystique of the Fokker Scourge, much discussed in RFC mess halls and eventually even in Great Britain's Parliament itself. Thus ,the overall effect of the Fokker fighters was much more

in terms of providing abundant newspaper and magazine propaganda opportunities in promoting the new German aces and their victories over the enemy than in actual number of aircraft downed.

The resultant loss in morale of the RFC airmen as they realized that they had no aircraft available to them with which to battle the new German fighter was also significant and the British aviators began referring to themselves as Fokker Fodder!

A more graphic example of the Fokker's effect on the RFC is provided by none other than Sir Hugh "Boom" Trenchard (see chapter No Empty Chairs) who was appointed to the command of the RFC on 19 August 1915. Trenchard was resolute in his belief that the RFC should be an offensive weapon and take the fight to the Germans over the trenches and behind their lines. The German command, not wanting to allow the secret of their new weapon to "escape" to the Allies, had forbidden the Fokker pilots to fly behind the Allied trenches. Thus, the Germans flew a defensive strategy which likely inhibited the overall possible effect of the Fokker fighters.

In addition, the Fokkers were, as mentioned,

Above: A photo of relaxed and high-spirited Fokker pilots.

Above: Ltn. Kurt Freiherr von Crailsheim in his Fokker as a member of Fokkerstaffel Monthois. He is a perfect example of the fact that most of the victories during the Fokker Scourge were scored by a relatively few pilots. He would gain a single victory on 7 September 1916 but would die from the injuries he suffered in a crash on 30th December.

Right: Lt. Kurt Wintgens was one of the more successful Fokker fighter pilots. He would be the fourth aviator to receive the PLM.

only sent to squadrons in groups of 1-3 total, and so their ability to capture air superiority over a given section of the trenches was significantly handicapped. Also, it was not until the spring of 1916 that the German air command re-organized the fighters into specific small units with the purpose of fighter missions alone: the so called Kampfeinsitzer Kommando (KEK).

Irrespective of the overall strategy concerning how best to deploy the aircraft, the pilots of the Fokker aircraft would work on improving their tactics while engaging the enemy. They developed what became known as the bounce where a German fighter pilot would gain as much altitude as possible to begin his mission, and when an enemy plane was sighted, the pilot would then maneuver his plane so that the sun would be in the eyes of the enemy and he would then dive to the attack.

If he was not able to shoot down the Allied plane on his first firing pass, the German fighter pilot would then use his extra speed from the dive to "zoom" back up to the advantage of the higher altitude and plan to repeat the attack. The pilot could also then change direction at the higher altitude in order to gain a better approach, a maneuver that has over time come to be called an Immelmann turn although it is unlikely that he

Above: Wintgens scored almost all of his victories in a Fokker monoplane, a type he seemed to prefer over the newer Halberstadt biplanes. His loyalty to the Fokker fighter ended in tragedy on the 25th September 1916 when Wintgens died while still flying in his Fokker E IV: he was pounced upon and shot down by French ace Alfred Heurtaux of escadrille N.3 who was flying one of the first examples of the new Spad VII.

Above: A clear sign of respect is shown by Oblt. Kurt Student, the commander of the Fokkerstaffel assigned to AOK 3. He re-purposed the Nieuport 11 of Lt. Jean Raty from N.38, which he had forced to land on 6 July 1916, with a synchronized Spandau machine gun and flew the aircraft in combat. Jasta 1 ace Gustav Leffers also sidelined his Fokker fighter and flew a captured Nieuport 16 in order to achieve his 7th victory over a RFC FE2b of No. 23 Sqdn.

"invented" such a maneuver, but merely utilized what other pilots had been doing for some time already.

Despite being hampered by their command's strategy, the successes of the Fokker pilots would dramatically affect the tactics of the RFC and forced the aggressive Trenchard to issue the following directive:

"Until the Royal Flying Corps is in possession of a machine as good as, or better than, the German Fokker, it seems that a change in policy and tactics has become necessary"

1) Every reconnaissance machine must be escorted by three other machines
2) All machines must fly in a close, escort type formation
3) Mission should NOT be continued if ANY of the machines becomes detached!"

This redefinition of RFC tactics was a major admission by such a figure as Trenchard. Thus, the overall effect of the Fokker monoplanes was far more than any actual tally of successes would eventually indicate.

At the peak of the Fokker Scourge in the late autumn of 1915 and into the winter of 1915/16, there were approximately 75 Fokker monoplanes on the front lines (23 of the latest E.III type) and yet an analysis of the RFC losses from July 1915 until December 1915 reveal the following:

- 84 aircraft lost
- 28 claims by Fokker pilots (some against French units)
- 13 of the Fokker claims were by either Boelcke or Immelmann!

Therefore, one of the lesser understood effects of the Fokker pilots was that their mere existence seemed to significantly bolster their comrade's morale and installed a more aggressive approach for those aircrew who were flying in other types of aircraft. The two-seater units now had the observer/gunner in position behind the pilot with a much better field of fire for his parabellum machine gun (also with 500+ rounds of ammunition available).

The overall success against Allied aircraft during the Fokker Scourge was thus also, in no small measure, attributable to the offensive minded flying of the two-seater aviators as well!

It also seems that the preponderance of aerial victories coming from the Fokker pilots would be skewed towards only the very top scoring pilots and not be spread evenly amongst the pilots, many of the Fokker pilots would score one or two victories if any at all.

Another key factor in limiting the overall success of the Fokker monoplane fighters was simply the relatively few number that were produced before the type was outclassed by newer Allied fighter types. Of the total number of Fokker monoplane fighters that were produced, the number that reached the Western Front was also never a high enough number to exert a profound influence towards air superiority, a rough estimate of the various versions, along with the prime differences in the types of the Fokker monoplane fighters follows:

- E.I 80 hp Oberursel rotary engine, unknown but likely "very few"
- EII, (100 hp Oberursel rotary engine) beginning in Sept. 1915, 23 total
- E.III (wing moved to lower connection point with fuselage) approximately 150
- E. IV (two machine guns and 160hp two-row rotary engine) in early 1916, approximately 40

In the end, there would be a total of 11 Fokker monoplane aces (scores while flying the Fokker monoplane only) during the approximately year long front line deployment of the Fokker monoplane variants (August 1915 to sometime in September 1916). As stated earlier, the majority of the Fokker monoplanes' successes came from the hands of only a few pilots:

Boelcke	18 victories
Immelmann	15 victories
Wintgens	16 victories
Mulzer	10 victories

By the end of 1915, the French had the superior Nieuport 11 fighter on the front lines, utilizing it to gain air supremacy during the Battle of Verdun. And by the winter of 1915/1916 the British had several squadrons of the capable Fe2 on the front lines, followed in March, 1916 by the DH 2 fighter which quickly established if not outright supremacy, a clear capacity to take the fight to their German counterparts. The brief but well-discussed, by Germans and Allies alike, aerial supremacy wrought by the Fokker monoplane fighters had come to its end.

In August, 1916 a German pilot became lost and accidentally landed his Fokker E.III at a British aerodrome. This was the first example of a Fokker monoplane that the Allies had captured. The aircraft was extensively flown and evaluated with the result that the relative modest performances of the aircraft were exposed, putting a final and definitive end to any concerns that the Allies had previously held regards the German Fokker menace.

However by this time the Fokker aircraft were being replaced by new biplanes built by Fokker, Albatros and Halberstadt aircraft firms: so a new chapter of the changing battle for control of the skies above the Western Front was already underway.

Perhaps the best epitaph for the episode in First World War aviation history known as the Fokker Scourge was written by a German, the 44 victory ace, Rudolf Berthold as quoted by the pre-eminent aviation historian Greg van Wyngarden in his book *Early German Aces of WWI*:

"We had too few qualified monoplanes – we lacked an aircraft that was easily maneuverable in combat. We had fallen asleep on the laurel wreaths that the single-seaters in the hands of a few superlative pilots had achieved. It was not the monoplane itself, but the pilots who were responsible for the success. One need but compare the number of Fokker fighters at the Front with those few pilots who had victories. I had already requested a new type of aircraft in January 1916 – a small biplane. People laughed!

The Frenchman, meanwhile, takes our experience to heart, quietly builds small biplanes and then launches hundreds at once against our lines. He has achieved air superiority and, with grinding teeth, we must watch while he shoots down our monoplanes and we're totally helpless." [p.55]

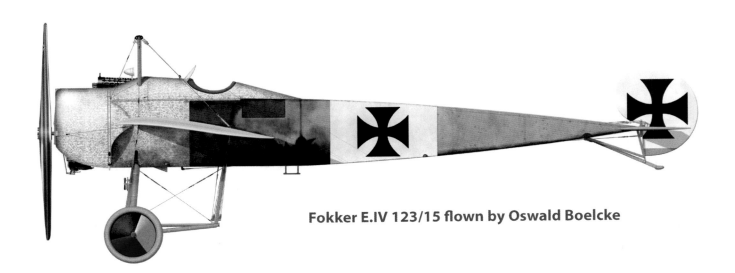

Fokker E.IV 123/15 flown by Oswald Boelcke

No Empty Chairs

Above: Group photo from the Central Flying School in 1913, Trenchard is seated third from right.

" ...the implacable determination of the Royal Flying Corps to pursue the offensive no matter what cost. Every one of its pilots was well aware that to practice the doctrine of attack day in, day out, meant losses, and if the enemy were as skillful and resolute...that those losses would be heavy. They were accepted without flinching. The mood of the officers and men of the Royal Flying Corps can be best depicted by a phrase used a generation later to describe the British people in a crisis even graver. They were grim and gay. The first quality was displayed in the air, the second in the Mess. However many empty chairs there might be, the spirit of relaxation, which tradition decreed must prevail after toil, was never allowed to depart from the board." Hilary St. George Saunders, written in 1944.

One of the most enduring stories of First World War aviation history, that has been studied in many different ways, is the concept of the Trenchard doctrine. Despite the brave words and images of the implacable British airmen that Saunders envisioned in 1944, the truth of the matter in 1916-1917 was not quite the same. During the Battle of the Somme, Trenchard was very worried about the possibility of

his aircrews becoming demoralized by the appalling losses they were suffering at the hands of the German fighter pilots.

Lost aircrew were rapidly replaced from a pool of newly trained pilots and observers who waited at the large RFC base at St. Omer for orders to report to frontline units. Trenchard explained this part of his strategy:

"A full breakfast table, with no empty chairs...If as an ordinary pilot you see no vacant places around you, the tendency is to brood less on the fate of friends who have gone forever. Instead your mind is taken up with buying drinks for the newcomers and making them feel at home."

Trenchard would not consider a diminished number of offensive missions, he would not consider a lessening of his aggressive tactics at any point in time. This resulted in RFC aircrew who were the product of abbreviated and faulty training being rushed into battle using inferior and inadequate aircraft to face a confident, experienced and well-equipped enemy. The results were hardly surprising. However, it would be wrong to write-off Trenchard as uncaring towards his men or unthoughtful regarding his strategy of offensive patrols constantly over the German lines.

In 1912, Major Hugh "Boom" Trenchard had:

"...become a rather lonely and discontented figure, approaching forty, unmarried and too unclubbable and poor for much higher rank. He was urged by a friend who had joined the just formed Royal Flying Corps to learn to fly and become a military pilot." Ian Mackersey

Trenchard did so and earned his Royal Aero Club pilot's certificate after only 64 minutes of actual flying time. In the end, his logbook would record a total of only 91 total flying hours in his career! However, he was convinced that the aeroplane would prove to be of enormous benefit to the army in any upcoming conflict.

He would become known as a very strict and stern leader with a lethal tongue that brokered no criticism or perceived sense of weakness within his command. An Air Mechanic named Cecil King remembered: "We were all a little bit scared of him because he was very severe and his manner quite frightening."

The tiny contingent of the Royal Flying Corps that was with the BEF in its retreat from the Mons proved itself to be useful and so overcame the enormous pre-war bias within the army that the aviators were frivolous and unneeded:

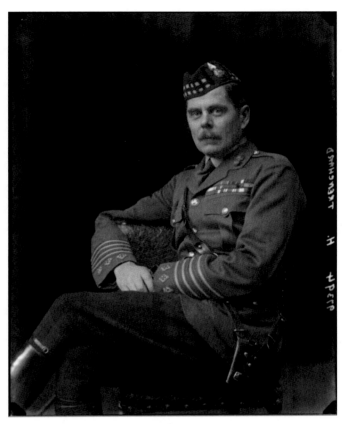

Above: A formal portrait of Hugh Trenchard.

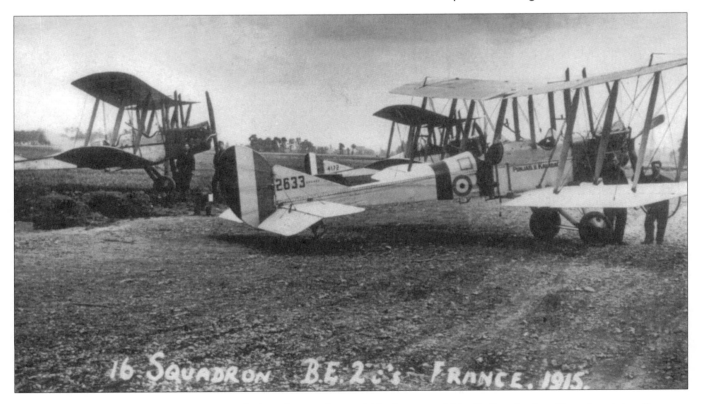

Above: BE2's of No. 16 squadron, although this photo is from 1915, there would be Be2 variants with only minimally changed flight characteristics serving in the front lines into the middle half of 1917.

A BE2 over the front lines.

Modern reproduction aircraft in New Zealand show the similarities of the BE2c and BE2e designs.

Above: A portrait of Fl. Sgt. W.G. Bennett dramatically captures the image of hundreds of RFC airmen like him. William Orpen was a well-respected Irish, painter who became a war artist for the British military in the First World War. Collection of the IWM.

Above: Another portrait by Orpen, Lt. R.T.C. Hoidge of 56 squadron RFC. Collection of IWM.

Below: One of the many young pilots of the RFC.

Above: Another pilot as photographed by his observer in the front seat.

"I wish particularly to bring to your Lordship's notice the admirable work done by the Royal Flying Corps under Sir David Henderson. Their skill, energy and perseverance have been beyond all praise. They have furnished me with complete and accurate information which has been of incalculable value in the conduct of operations...they have remained undaunted throughout." Sir John French, commander of the BEF

The newest branch of the army thus established its own traditions at the very start of the First World War: no request from the army was to go unanswered and no assessment of its dangers would be able to prevent the mission from going forward.

An often overlooked fact is that during the First World War, the various German positions along the Western Front were chosen by them and were inevitably in superior locations of high ground opposite the British forces.

Many military historians have discussed that the First World War was, in its most edited form, a war of artillery forces. Thus, the German artillery observers could direct their fire from the various viewing posts along the front lines and could see the

results as the shells struck the Allied lines.

However, for the British to have any kind of effective artillery fire, the RFC's Corps observation aircraft had to be above the German lines/ target positions and relay the needed information in order to direct a successful artillery "shoot".

To be compatible with the offensive-minded strategy of the British High Command, the RFC was essentially forced into taking an offensive approach and put its airmen/aircraft over German-held territory. These actions were well-tailored to fit into the German concept of fighting its air war in a defensive manner. There would be, almost always, fewer German aircraft available to match-up against the Allied air units anywhere along a specific sector of the front lines.

Although the German commanders would concentrate their air units in the most active spots along the front lines, they typically remained outnumbered. In addition, the Germans were forced to be "risk averse" in their planning, since they realized that they could not keep up if their losses in either aircraft or aircrew proved to be too high.

Therefore the German commanders began to

Above: The FE8 could take on the Fokker monoplanes in a more than even fashion; however, by the time it reached the front lines it would have to battle newer German designs. Steve Anderson

concentrate their aircraft into small, mobile units that could be moved where needed and grouped together in smaller sections of the front lines where the fighting was at the highest levels: in an attempt to gain temporary control of the air.

To gain air superiority, the Germans were greatly aided by having superior aircraft, and now coupled with the experienced fighter pilots in those cockpits, it was a combination that would prove deadly during the war: especially during several key battles.

Keeping in mind that from the summer of 1915 leading into the Battle of the Somme in July 1916, the British aviation units were flying BE 2, DH 2 and FE 2 aircraft against the German Fokker monoplane fighters. Then from the Fall of 1916 leading into the Battle of Arras in April, 1917 the British squadrons were flying essentially the same aircraft against the next generation of vastly improved German fighter aircraft, which included the Albatros-D types.

In the fall of 1916, a new British fighter was sent to the front, another pusher aircraft the Fe8 was meant to improve upon the DH 2. Regrettably for the pilots forced to fly the aircraft, it was designed to combat the Fokker monoplanes that were now being removed from front line service and would prove to be vastly out-performed by the German Albatros and Halberstadt fighters it would end up fighting. Still, No. 40 and 41 squadrons were sent to the front lines in the fall of 1916 and continued to fly the type into the following spring!

An example of the inequity in combat faced by the Fe8 pilots, on 9th March 1917 9 Fe8's engaged 8 Albatros DII fighters (led by von Richthofen) with the result that four of the Fe8's were shot down and another four were badly damaged, barely making it back to the British side of the front lines.

Another "remedy" for the Fokker scourge was the BE 12 "fighter", which was essentially a Be2c

Above: Although a photo taken by a gun camera during training, this image is likely what many German fighter pilots saw on the Western Front from 1915–1917.

Below: An evocative image of the men of No. 32 Squadron, RFC, July 1916.

Above: The Albatros D.I shown here was the pre-eminent fighter type over the Western Front upon its introduction in the autumn of 1916 : variants of the type, the D.II and D.III, would continue the types successful prowess until the summer of 1917. Art courtesy of Roden models.

that had one cockpit removed and was armed with a Lewis gun firing from its top wing. This aircraft was a profound failure form its inception and was immediately re-designated a "light tactical bomber". Inadequate aircraft designs were only one problem for Trenchard as he attempted to maintain control of the air.

A significant, further problem for Trenchard as he tried to meet the army's demands with the units he had on hand:

"The flow of newly trained aircrew from England was barely keeping up with the Fokker casualties. And there weren't enough competent instructors to teach the pilot recruits to fly properly. Some were arriving in France with so little experience they were a menace to their squadrons, wrecking their machines before they even crossed the lines." Ian Mackersey

The deadly mix of inferior and inadequate aircraft, coupled with abbreviated training by inadequate instructors was the foundation upon which Trenchard's avowed policy of aggressive tactics along with his unwillingness to retreat from daily, constant offensive missions was to be built.

The results lead to the concept of a "Fokker Scourge" and that the aircrew were mere "Fokker Fodder" being bantered about during the late summer of 1915 and even into 1916. The despair even led to Noel Pemberton-Billing, speaking in the House of Commons, to state that the RFC pilot's were being "rather murdered than killed".

The commander of the RFC, Sir David Henderson was not unaware of the problems and was himself working through innumerable challenges. An exchange with his commander in France (Trenchard) in March 1916 revealed some of his frustrations:

"We cannot send out the squadrons promised this month and at the same time keep you up to strength in pilots" he[Henderson] wrote…"I am sorry for this but the combination of bad weather and casualties has brought us down for the moment to bedrock in pilots." Trenchard replied: "I am, as you say, frightfully worried over the loss of pilots out here. You can imagine it is not quite an easy game at present."

As an example of what RFC front line squadrons were facing, consider No. 60 squadron which was

86

Above: An Albatros D.II flown by German ace Josef Jacobs, whose nickname was *Kobes,* attacks a French bombing formation. Note that the pusher aircraft are trying to form and maintain a defensive circle so that they can "cover" each others vulnerable tail position from attack. Steve Anderson.

Above: The BE12 was a wholly inadequate design as a fighter; it was essentially a BE2 with the front cockpit removed and a more powerful engine than the BE2 variants. It proved hopeless against the German fighters.

Right: Another hopeful British fighter, the FE8, was designed to counter the Fokker monoplane. However, it did not arrive at the front lines until August 1916 and was far outclassed by the German Albatros and Halberstadt designs that were arriving at the frontat that time.

88

Above: A 41 Squadron FE8 in flight.

Above: German Albatros D.II fighters of Jasta 9 prepare to take off.

Above: American John Ruskin Watts is about to become the Kaiser's "guest" for the remainder of the war. Mike O'Neal.

sent to the front in July 1916. This squadron was equipped with Morane Saulnier monoplanes and biplanes, some of the fastest aircraft the RFC had at the time, and the squadron was intended to be a fighter squadron that would aggressively take on the Fokker monoplanes. Expert RFC historian Alex Revell states:

"In a month of operations, No. 60 Sqdn. had suffered 12 casualties. Smith-Barry was appalled. He was convinced that many were the result of the inadequate training of his replacement pilots... informed Trenchard, who telephoned Haig of his decision to withdraw the squadron from active duty."

Just who were these young men, ever so eager to get into "the game":

"The biggest pool of Flying Corps recruits were eager English public schoolboys. Undeterred by the sensational coverage of the Fokker carnage, many were cutting short their education and falsifying their ages to join up before the war ended and denied them their romantic adventure. The ethos of the RFC was firmly public school, Its squadrons, at least initially[until the losses were too severe], were elite establishments in which grammar-school, lower-middle and, most emphatically, working-class applicants found scant welcome." Ian Mackersey

Lt. Sholto Douglas, from Oxford University himself, transferred from the Royal Horse Artillery into the RFC at about this time and found:

"After the rigid discipline that I had known in the Royal Horse Artillery the free and easy way in which things were done in the RFC was very much to my liking...they were men of a different breed

Above: The Albatros D.I and D.II designs were a tremendous step forward in fighter aircraft design: fast, rugged, and armed with two machine guns and 1,000 rounds of ammunition, the type was flown to incredible success by the German front-line fighter pilots.

from what I had been accustomed...I was now in the company of individualists, some of whom, I was soon to find, could even be regarded as at least eccentrics- if not downright crazy."

An RFC pilot, Arthur Gould Lee wrote in his memoirs after the war (*NO PARACHUTE*):

"Almost the only light that shone during the long period of neglect, incompetence and folly in the supply of aircraft to the RFC was the undismayed courage of those sent out every day to face death in aeroplanes that should have been thrown on the scrapheap many months before."

Cecil Lewis, another RFC pilot of this time who wrote the superb *SAGITTARIUS RISING* after the war had this observation from his aircraft:

"The war below us was a spectacle. We aided and abetted it, admiring the tenacity of men who fought in verminous filth to take the next trench thirty yards away. But such objectives could not thrill us, who, when we raised our eyes, could see objective after objective receding, fifty, sixty, seventy miles beyond. Indeed, the fearful thing about the war became its horrible futility, the mountainous waste of life and wealth to stake a mile or two of earth. There was so much beyond. Viewed with detachment, it had all the elements of grotesque comedy- a prodigious and complex effort, cunningly contrived and carried out with deadly seriousness, in order to achieve just nothing at all."

Yet the RFC achieved much more than they were

Above: A Jasta 16 Albatros D.II in flight. Compare its apparent aerodynamics to the photo of the FE 8 in flight.

Right: 2/Lt. John Ruskin Watts was an American volunteer in the RFC. Unfortunately for him, his first (and last) front-line aircraft was a BE12.

giving themselves credit for. The commander of the German First Army along the Somme, General Fritz von Below wrote:

"With the aid of aeroplane observation the hostile artillery neutralized our guns and was able to range with most extreme accuracy on the trenches occupied by our infantry...the enemy's aircraft inspired our troops with a feeling of defenselessness."

As if the Fokker Scourge was not bad enough, in the spring of 1917 the British launched yet another major offensive and the Battle of Arras began. Again, the RFC was tasked with flying reconnaissance missions to find the critical targets and then to take on the hazardous missions of directing artillery fire onto those targets.

In addition, the low-flying RFC crews would be tasked with contact patrols to find where the infantry units were actually located during the battle. All the time, the aircrew were exposed to ground fire and even though they were flying in the same aircraft as the previous year; they were now facing the newly organized Jastas in their even more superior Albatros and Halberstadt fighter aircraft.

As the air battles of April 1917 were underway, a month that would become known in history as Bloody April because of the staggering losses suffered by the RFC crews on the front lines, Trenchard wrote to RFC commanding staff in England:

"My dear Brancker, We are fighting a very big battle and the fighting in the air is becoming intense, and will increase, I regret to say, not decrease. It is only a question of our keeping it going longer than the Huns. If we cannot do that then we are beaten; if we do it then we win...I must warn you now that in the next ten days if we get fine weather I anticipate a very heavy casualty list. There are many more German machines, fast and much better fighters which have suddenly appeared on our front opposite to us than there have been before. I hope you will take this letter very seriously and take stock of how we shall be off for pilots this autumn and the larger number of casualties we are bound to have."

An example of just what was happening can be found in what the commanding officer of No. 60 squadron(again) wrote:

"From the last week in March to the last week in May our losses were very severe...We lost 35 officers during those eight weeks, almost twice the strength of the squadron. One weekend in April was especially unlucky. On Saturday A flight went out six machines strong and only one returned. On Monday C flight went out and only one returned. In three days ten out of eighteen pilots were lost and had to be replaced from England by officers who had never flown this type of machine- because there were none in England."

Facing such staggering losses, the surviving pilots seemed to have felt like Ira Jones when he wrote the following:

"This aggressively offensive spirit could not tolerate sorrow, for sorrow was liable to lower morale. Though it might hide in the bosom of the pilot, it was only permitted to exude in the secret seclusion of his sleeping quarters. In the mess it was an unwritten law for pilots to forget the sorrow and assume a cheerfulness which gave the impression to the casual visitor of 'living for the day'. Thus was morale maintained at an unusually high level... Without such a tradition the strongest of spirits would soon break under the excessive nervous strain of terrifying combats and personal losses."

The RFC was losing almost 200 pilots a month in the spring of 1917 and at one point the average life expectancy of a front line RFC pilot was 11 days. Yet, the pilots and observers in the RFC persevered. They did not waver from their commitment and did not shirk from their duty.

A wonderful example of this attitude and the enormous expenditures required was 2/Lt. John Ruskin Watts. A native of Westfield, New Jersey he joined the RFC via Canada in April, 1916. Upon arrival in the European Theatre he was initially a ferry pilot bringing aircraft from England to France. Eventually he was assigned to No. 19 squadron and made his first operational flight on the 14th October 1916. He was flying a Be 12 aircraft as an escort "fighter" on the 22nd October as he joined his comrades on a bombing mission to attack German positions around Louveral, Belgium. This mission would take them 50 kilometers from their airfield at Fienviller and would necessitate them flying far behind German lines.

Their flight path also brought them a mere 3 kilometers from Lagnicourt, where the aerodrome for Jasta 2 was located. Boelcke led von Richthofen and others in an attack which fairly decimated the British formation. Flying their new and deadly Albatros D.II fighters , the Germans had no trouble in dominating the dogfight. OffStv. Reimann scored his fifth victory when he downed the BE12 flown by Watts. A mere eight days after his first operational flight, Watts was brought down and captured – he would spend the remainder of the war as a POW.

Again and again, courageous young airmen carried on through 1915, 1916 and well-into 1917: buying the time needed until the RFC would become the RAF and with new, better aircraft and better training for its pilots, would prove to be the formidable force that continued the offensive spirit , the Trenchard doctrine, into 1918 and onto ultimate victory.

Until that victory, there was a long-painful time in history that was captured by the words of Cecil Lewis:

"A moment came when even the most supremely self-confident aces began to wonder when their turn would come. You sat down to dinner faced by the empty chairs of men you had laughed and joked with at lunch. They were gone. The next day new men would laugh and joke from those chairs. Some might be lucky and stick it for a bit, some chairs would be empty very soon. And so it would go on. And always, miraculously, you were still there. Until tomorrow."

Above: A modern reproduction of a BE2 evokes the spirit of the British airmen of 1915–1917.

Right: William Orpen's portrait of H. Trenchard was done in May, 1917: just after the disastrous month known as "Bloody April". Collection of IWM.

Anatomy of a Fighter Aircraft

Above: An original color photo shows French ace Sgt. Jean Chaput of escadrille N. 57 in April 1916, beside his newly arrived Nieuport 11.

The courageous young men who flew into the beginnings of aerial warfare did so in the most modern and advanced aircraft of their time. With that said, the types of aircraft that were utilized were often dangerous and frail in many ways. Most of the aircraft designs were made with the best intentions possible, however it must be remembered that the science of aerodynamics and the skilled engineering along with the required mathematical calculations that would be eventually needed for safe aircraft design were still in the future.

As discussed elsewhere, the military aircraft that were on the frontlines in 1914, were obsolete and museum relics by the time the war ended in 1918 (although some designs such as the Bleroit and the Caudron were still being utilized as early pilot training aircraft).

Rapid changes to the aircraft being produced and sent into combat thus makes it hard to avoid over-generalizations as one considers what was a typical First World War fighter aircraft really like.

Mark Miller has made some incredible computer generated images of several prominent and common types of First World War fighters that are works of art themselves. His work puts a draftsman-like skill that reveals the work of the skilled laborers that built the aeroplanes. His talented efforts also reveal what was essentially a work of art in itself: the hand built fighter aircraft of World War I.

Gustave Delage became the chief designer of aeroplanes at the French firm Nieuport in January, 1914. He worked on developing a pre-war racing design. Up to that point, the Nieuport designs were monoplanes but Delage envisioned a sleek, biplane design. His biggest contribution to aircraft design was making his biplane what would become known as a sesquiplane design.

Up to that time, all biplanes had two wings of equal length and span, The Nieuport concept would be that the lower wing was of much smaller size, a wing-and-a half so to speak. The narrower lower wing certainly allowed for better overall pilot vision. More importantly though, the smaller lower wing drastically reduced the aircraft's overall drag and

since the lower wing was less important in regards to lift, the trade off was a big positive for the Nieuport design.

The upper wing was quite conventional with widely spaced spars, full chord ribs that were cross-braced with wire. The ribs featured cut outs to lighten the overall weight.

The fuselage featured ash longerons that tapered from the engine mount wall back towards the rudder post, braced with internal wires and struts.

These "bones" of the aircraft were then covered in stretched linen which was tacked and glued in place. Then the linen was stiffened with a dope or lacquer to make the surface stable and aerodynamic.

The position of the engine, oil and fuel tanks were immediately in front of or in some designs below the pilot seat so as to keep the center of gravity forward and to improve the acrobatic handling of the aircraft.

Thus, the pilots would be sitting behind a rapidly spinning rotary engine, which spewed castor oil lubricant backwards in the slipstream, while the flammable wood and doped linen construction awaited any flame to incinerate itself – fueled by

gasoline stored in close proximity to the pilot! Again, remember the pilot had no parachute. No wonder that on occasion pilots would talk about being in flammable coffins.

The most dangerous, inherent flaw in the Nieuport design was in its lower wing which was connected to the fuselage by a single spar. Its attachment was behind the center of lift, which therefore would cause the risk of flutter at high speeds which could cause the wing to separate from the airplane.

This aerodynamic concept was not yet understood and in fact, writing after the war, Leonard Bridgman in The Clouds Remember wrote:

" It is probable that this fault did develop on at least one occasion, but whether as a result of any inherent defect in the design, or for some other reason it is impossible to say."

Thus, it should be remembered that the aviators of the First World War of all air services took to the air in aircraft designs that had yet to be fully and properly tested since the overall knowledge of aeronautical engineering and the understanding of aircraft design were still unfolding as the war was

Mark Miller's fabulous work displays the
"anatomy" of a Nieuport fighter. Mark Miller

fought. Bridgeman also wrote:

"Like other French single-seaters the Nieuport Scout was exceedingly pleasant to fly and very handy on the controls...For 'dog-fighting' of the most intensive kind, when aeroplanes whirled about within inches of each other, it is doubtful if there was ever a better machine than the Nieuport Scout."

Certainly Albert Ball believed that to be true. When Ball was heading back to the Western Front as a flight commander in the newly formed No. 56 squadron flying the brand new S.E. 5, he personally petitioned the R.F.C. commander Hugh Trenchard to be allowed a personal Nieuport Scout to fly because he preferred the diminutive, rotary-engined acrobatic fighter to the inline engined S.E. 5.

Nieuport aircraft served in every single Allied air service and served from the very beginning

until the end of the war. From the early Nieuport 10 , then types 11, 12, 16, 17, 21, 23 and even onto the 27 fighters the overall design is immediately recognizable. Eventually wIngs grew in span, overall aircraft size and weight got much larger as bigger, more powerful Le Rhone and Clerget rotary engines effectively dictated the needed changes.

No matter what the type, the Nieuport fighters were generally enthusiastically received by their pilots and could hold their own in dogfights against their German adversaries because of their maneuverability.

By the fall of 1916, the German AIr Service was losing control of the skies as their Fokker monoplanes became outmatched by the Nieuport 11 and the D.H.2 and F.E.2 designs. The answer for how to recover their aerial supremacy came from

Miller's display of an Albatros D.V fighter shows the smooth plywood-covered, semi-monocoque fuselage design invented by Hugo Grohmann. The model adopted the Nieuport wing cellule and inherited the structural problems associated with the single-spar lower wing. Mark Miller

Miller highlights the thick, cantilever wings – Fokker's aerodynamic and structural breakthrough – and lack of drag-inducing rigging in his Fokker D.VII image; compare to the interior photo of a D.VII cockpit. Fokker's innovative wing design was key to the great success of the Fokker D.VII, arguably the best fighter of the war. Mark Miller

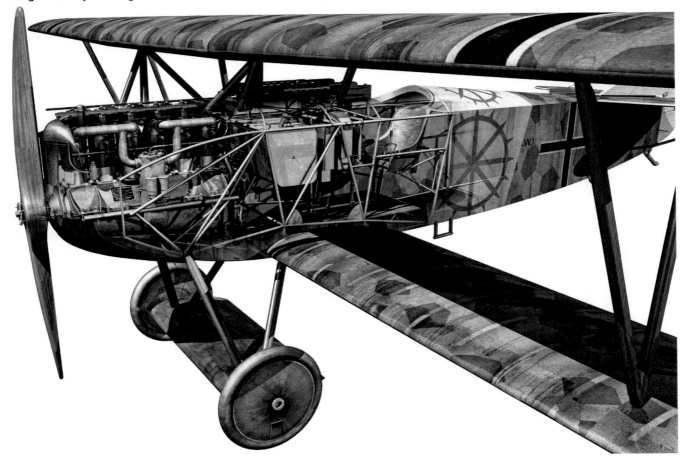

Above: An early Nieuport 17 in a demonstration flight at Le Breguet airport.

Above: An original color photo of a Nieuport fighter of escadrille N.77 in the winter of 1916–1917, the pilot is unidentified.

Above: An original color photo of a Nieuport 23. The machine gun is a synchronized Vickers.

Above: An RFC Nieuport taking off; note the need for ground crew to help with stabilizing the aircraft on the ground.

Above: American Courtney Campbell of the Escadrille Lafayette survived a flight following the loss of one of his lower wings, a not rare event if the aircraft was flown in high-g maneuvers, especially for Nieuports with their single-spar lower wing. Albatros "V-strutters" inherited the same problem from using the Nieuport wing cellule.

Above: A replica Sopwith Pup aircraft demonstrates the common "skeleton" of a WWI fighter. Two spars were used in all wings, avoiding the weakness of the Nieuport single-spar lower wing.

the militarization of a pre-war racing design of the Albatros works.

The Albatros-Flugzeugwerke GmbH was founded in 1909 by Walter Huth and Otto Wiener in Berlin-Johannisthal. Initially the company built license-approved models of Taubes and Farman aircraft.

One of their designers, Robert Thelan conceived

of what many aviation historians credit as the first true fighter aircraft. His Albatros D. I was sleek, fast and able to mount two forward-firing machine guns and would immediately out perform its Allied opponents by a large measure.

The Fokker monoplane was the first aircraft to mount a machine gun, but it was an

Above: An Albatros D.III in flight, displaying the sesquiplane design copied from the Nieuport. The higher aspect ratio sesquiplane wings improved speed and climb over the otherwise identical D.II at the cost of fragile lower wings.

underperforming design and was a pre-war sporting design that simply had a gun attached.

Considering its overall design, the Albatros was unique for its day because of its semi-monocoque fuselage, which was of all-wood construction. The unequal-span wings were also different in design, but constructed of a typical wooden framework that was covered by fabric. It had a very distinctive empenagge that would never significantly change in any of the forthcoming various types.

Its overall appearance was shark-like, certainly it appeared to look like a fighter aircraft.

By the time it was being readied for front line use, synchronized guns were available and the Albatros was purposely modified to become an effective fighter aircraft. The German fighter pilots became more confident and aggressive with the arrival of the Albatros D.I and D.II types.

Even as they were gaining control of the skies against their foes, the German pilots reported a generally held respect for their opponents and how they could maneuver their Nieuport fighters in a dogfight. After test flights of various, captured Nieuport types the Albatros company was given a directive to re-design its Albatros fighter and the D.III type was born.

The biggest change to the D.III was that the upper wing was made slightly larger and the lower wing was now changed to a sesquiplane design-copied directly from the Nieuport fighter.

The D.III thus inherited the lower wing flutter problem and many field modifications would follow in an attempt to eliminate the problem. Eventually, the Oeffag company of Wiener-Neustadt built their own re-designed (modified) Albatros for the Austro-Hungarian AIr Service which would serve well and would overcome the inherent defects in the sesquiplane design.

The jagdstaffeln swiftly put their new fighters to good use. The Albatros D.I, D.II and D.III types would all serve together for much of 1917 and would lead to their tremendously successful "Bloody April" against the RFC during the Battle of the Somme. The types D.V/V.a would follow, although they would not really be much improvement upon the early types.

Albatros fighters would be used not only over the Western Front, but the Eastern Front, in Italy and even Palestine: essentially they would face off against their opponents in Nieuport fighters in every theatre of the war.

As 1917 led to 1918, the Allied fighter pilots

Above: A modern Albatros replica in flight.

began to reassert themselves in the cockpits of their Spads, SE 5s and Sopwith Camels. Manfred von Richthofen himself offered his opinion of the status of the Albatros fighters at the end of 1917: "[the Albatros] is so obsolete and so ridiculously inferior to the English that one cannot do anything with this aircraft."

Eventually, Albatros was ordered to halt the production of their design in February, 1918. The company was to begin the production of their rival's latest effort, the Fokker D.VII.

Left: Lothar von Richthofen is seated in his Albatros fighter and is in discussion with another German ace Ltn. Karl Schafer. Note the ladder against the side of the fuselage; the rounded Albatros fuselage made entry into the cockpit difficult, especially with heavy boots or coats that a pilot needed to stay warm. It was traditional to enter the aircraft from the left, similar to a cavalry member mounting his horse from the left.

Above: An Albatros D.V of Jasta 18; the D.V was not a noticeable improvement on the D.III and soon led to German aces asking for a better fighter design to combat the newer Allied designs.

The Fokker D.VII was the finest fighter and the most advanced aircraft design of the war. The aircraft type was specifically mentioned in the terms of the Armistice, the Allies required the Germans to turn over all examples of the airplane.

It featured Fokker's typical welded-steel tubing and incorporated a new concept, the cantilever wing. For most of the early days of aircraft design, the generally accepted belief was that wings needed to be thin in order to reduce drag. However, the thin wings necessitated the use of struts and multiple bracing wires to provide adequate strength to the design so as to withstand the g-forces that would be encountered in flight.

Now it is understood that the struts and bracing wires were the causes of excessive drag, and that the internal box spar construction of the thick wing was much more efficient. The thickened, cantilever wing resulted in more lift as well. The cantilever wing was actually the idea of Hugo Junkers, but Fokker "borrowed" the concept and then incorporated thin sheets of plywood instead of the more time-consuming, expensive corrugated metal that Junkers was working with in his design.

The wing's capability of high lift gave it an exceptionally docile handling during a stall. The Fokker was generally acknowledged as an aircraft that could make an average pilot a good pilot and a good pilot an ace.

The Fokker D.VII F was a variant that used the newly designed BMW IIIa engine and gave even more outstanding performance for the German fighter pilot to take advantage of. Because of the increased number of Fokker D.VIIs available towards the end of 1918, despite having much fewer total numbers of aircraft and having to ration their sorties per day because of a lack of fuel, the German fighter units continued to be a very dangerous foe.

The Germans also changed their tactics and utilized larger formations of fighter aircraft at one time, often utilizing a combination of aircraft from different Jastas in the same flight. In fact, in September 1918 (Black September for the RAF) 560 Allied aircraft were downed, compared to the loss of 300 aircraft during the Bloody April of 1917.

However, even with the most technically advanced fighter aircraft in the world and even with increased numbers of Allied aircraft shot down by using newer tactics and approaches, the Germans could not stop the Allies from gaining aerial supremacy and victory.

The Fokker DVII design was coveted for its strength and flying qualities and would serve in many air forces throughout the world into the late 1920's.

Above: A modern replica Fokker D.VII in flight shows the thick wing that gave the type some of its outstanding flight characteristics; note also the lack of rigging which dramatically reduced unwelcome drag.

Facing Page: Workers at the Albatros factory putting finishing touches on a license-built Fokker D.VII, in fact the Albatros factory-built Fokkers outnumbered those built by Fokker itself. Albatros produced more aircraft than any other German company partly because it had extensive production facilities, much bigger than the small Fokker facilities.

Below: Although First World War aircraft had inherent weaknesses, at times the robust design of struts and rigging of the two wings recapitulated the truss design of a bridge for example.

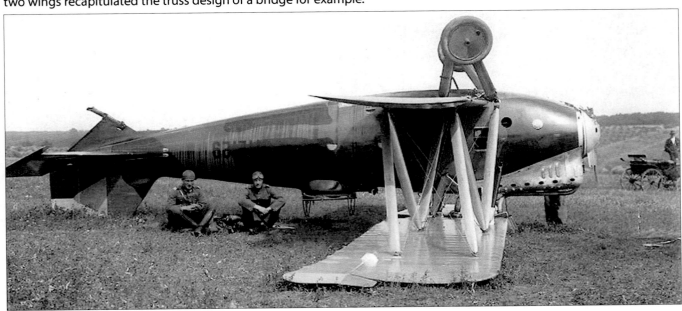

Above: An interior view of an original Fokker D.VII at the NASM: note the fabric fuselage sides and the inherently simple steel tubular fuselage design of Fokker aircraft, and the paucity of instruments.

The Nearsighted Ace

Above: Sometime near the start of the war, Belgian aviators beside a HF 20 observation aircraft. L to R: unknown, Jacquet, Paul Hiernaux, Felix Isserentant.

One of the best characteristics to have as a fighter ace is excellent vision. The observations that First World War pilots mentioned about each other would be replete with references to an ace having eagle vision: the descriptions of the most successful fighter aces would seem to help define a term that would come later in the annals of military aviation history: situational awareness.

That solitary two-seater observation aircraft that seemed to be a helpless prey just waiting for the fledgling fighter pilot to swoop upon, would often be a trap. As a group of enemy fighter aircraft would then pounce upon the hapless novice from a higher altitude, perhaps unseen as the flight hid in and out of clouds or had maneuvered themselves so as to attack from out of the sun.

The ability to see the enemy before they saw you, to see the threats that were constantly in the sky over the Western Front before those enemy aircraft could attack you was thus a tremendous, almost fundamental advantage.

Yet, one of the truly remarkable aces of the First World War was hopelessly near-sighted, his vision so bad that he flew the entire war in two-seater aircraft so as to have an observer/gunner who could watch out for enemy aircraft in the distance and would likely be able to see well enough to hit the enemy once engaged in combat.

Captain-Commandant Fernand Maximillian Leon Jacquet would become one of only five Belgian aces during the war. Jacquet had earned civil brevet #68 in 1913 and then gained his military wings in August 1913, thus joining the Compagnie d'Aviateurs before the war began.

108

Above: A MF11bis in flight.
Below: Jacquet and Robin in their MF11bis, in which they scored their 20 May 1916 victory.

Above: An Aviatik C-type aircraft of the type downed on the 20th May.

Below: Aviatik C.227 in the water off the coast, the second victory of Jaquet, the first victory for Robin, and the third victory of the AvM.

Above: Depicting the height of the dogfight on 20th May 1916 as Jacquet and Robin dive into a flight of German Aviatik biplanes and successfully shoot one down. Robert Karr

Thus, Jacquet found himself in the 1st escadrille at the start of the war and flew his first sortie on the 4th August 1914: which prematurely ended because of a faulty engine. Only two days later, Jacquet was in the air again and encountered a German Taube, which he naturally attacked: without success.

Because of the extremely limited capacity to attack his country's invaders in the sky, Jacquet would occasionally patrol the area around his aerodrome in a car driven by Prince de Caraman-Chimay while Jacquet would man a Lewis machine gun he brought along!

His first dogfight would end without victory on 26th February 1915, but Jacquet was only more incentivized to continue on the attack.

Only two days following the Frenchman Roland Garros's second victory, Jacquet would score his first confirmed victory and the first official victory for the Belgian Air Force on 17th April 1915 when he and his observer Lt. Henri Vindevoghel downed a German two-seater Albatros near Beerst.

The two would not again score a confirmed victory but that was not for the lack of trying:

- 20th June- attacked and claimed Aviatik out of control, not confirmed
- 21st June- engaged in two separate attacks on German aircraft without success
- 24th July- forced down an Aviatik near Westende, again unconfirmed
- 28th July- forced an Aviatik to land near Gits, unconfirmed
- 30th July- combat against an Aviatik, withdrew because of gun failure
- 31st July- 20 minute combat with German aircraft, inconclusive battle, Jacquet/ Vindevoghel landed at their aerodrome with an aircraft that was "riddled", their MF had to be struck off
- 5th Sept- Jacquet/ Vindevoghel were shot down after their engine was hit, they force landed near Pervyse
- 8th Sept- unsuccessful attack against a balloon near St.Pierre Capelle
- 13th Sept- Jacquet was wounded by shrapnel from AA fire, his aircraft had more than 30 hits

Therefore it would seem that Jacquet was shot down or returned with aircraft so damaged that the Belgian Air Force lost at least three aircraft versus the one confirmed victory he had obtained in 1915!

It would appear the Jacquet then had to take some time away from the front lines to recover from his wounds: but he would not be kept away from action for very long and now when he returned, he

Jacquet (note his eyeglasses) and Robin pose by their new GN 2; the GN1 and GN2 were developed from the Farman. The GN 2 modifications were made at the request of Jacquet and included a streamlined nacelle, reduced upper wing span, and a re-designed undercarriage to reduce drag. Chalk lines show where their insignia was to be painted.

Above: Jacquet prepares to take the Belgian King Albert aloft for a flight over the front lines on 18th March 1917. Lt. Robin holds the ladder steady.

Facing Page: Jacquet and Robin beside the same aircraft, now decorated with their La Sale Gueule or grinning skull.

Above: Jacquet and Robin in their GN 4 (note the Hispano-Suiza inline engine) shortly after scoring Jacquet's 3rd victory on 30th July 1916, also note the variation of the grinning skull.

had a new observer/gunner, Lt. Louis Marie Omer Auguste Robin. Robin has been described by the expert on Belgian aviation, Walter Pieters as "an aggressive man with a contempt of death".

Lt. Robin had been flying combat missions since March 1915 and on 29th September 1915 he flew with his pilot, sLt. Roger Castiau, over Brussels releasing a Belgian flag to flutter down onto the captured capital from their aircraft. They then flew over and released several small bombs on the Zeppelin base at Etterbeek.

Robin's brazen courageousness would prove to be an excellent match to Jacquet's own boundless urge to engage German aircraft. In fact, it was Jacquet's own brother who recommended Robin and the two promptly flew into the Flander's sky looking for trouble which would result in over 70 combats and three confirmed victories in 1916 for the pair.

It must be remembered that for much of the war, the German staff considered the approximately 60 km. of the Yser front as stalemated and were content with that situation. The German's considered the Belgian Air Force as a "negligible" threat and so allocated very few resources to the area until towards the second half of 1917.

Also slowing the successes of the duo of Jacquet and Robin is that they flew in slow, cumbersome pusher aircraft throughout 1916 and even into the spring of 1917. And still the two proved to be the aggressor again and again, with almost a fervent desire to punish the Germans for the invasion of their neutral country. Their typical tactic was to fly north and eastward over the North Sea and then as they achieved the altitude they wanted, the two would wait to dive upon an unsuspecting German aircraft that was headed back towards its airfield- they often achieved total surprise since their attack came from so deep from inside German-held territory.

- 1st May- an inauspicious start for the two, as they attacked a German LVG but suffered a gun jam and returned to their aerodrome "shot up"
- 20th May- Shot down Aviatik C.227/16 for Jacquet's 2nd victory/ Robin's 1st and the third official victory for the AvM.
- 26th May- attacked a LVG, then later engaged 3 Aviatiks, forcing one to land, unconfirmed
- 27th May- forced another Aviatik to land,

again unconfirmed

- 23rd June- in several combats during a single sortie, shot down a Fokker E-type for confirmed victory, fought another Fokker without success, engaged several enemy two seaters and finally returned to their aerodrome with their MF again "shot up"
- 30th June- after an extended dogfight, they forced the German Aviatik to land, unconfirmed
- 8th July- Big effort to bomb a German naval gun at Mariakerke. French MF 36, 1 Wing RNAS and four Belgian F40's were assigned to the attack: Jacquet and Robin flew toward the target even though they were not assigned the mission- they initially engaged a Fokker E-type and drove it off, then fought two LVG's, forcing one of them to land on a nearby beach, unconfirmed
- 9th July- the very next day the two fought 3 Aviatiks, 1LVG and another Fokker E-type, with the Fokker seen diving away out of control and although this fact was confirmed by another pilot, no confirmed victory was given
- 28th July- strafed enemy aircraft at Ghistelles airfield
- 30th July- the pair recorded their 8th claim, and scored Jacquet's fourth official victory by downing an Aviatik - the claim was "helped" when the two took a photo of their victim as proof!

The team of Jacquet and Robin simply flew every day they possibly could and this sampling of their actions clearly demonstrates their offensive minded spirits and their ceaseless attempts to seek out their enemies.

Finally, on the 1st of February 1917 , Jacquet and Robin (now flying in their Belgian modified GN 2 pusher aircraft, which was based on the French Farman F40) shot down a Rumpler from FA(A)213 for Jacquet's fifth confirmed victory- making him the first Belgian ace of the war!

Jacquet flew a very special mission on 18th March 1917, however for this mission Robin did not occupy his usual seat in their GN2. For this flight over the front lines, that seat would be occupied by King Albert himself, on his first flight over the front lines.

However, this successful team was broken apart when Lt. Robin was transferred to the 6me Escadrille on the 30th April. The transfer was apparently based on his impertinence to the commander of their escadrille, an altercation that lead to a physical fight. The escadrille's commander was transferred back to

his artillery unit, Robin was dispatched to another escadrille and Jacquet was ordered to fly his GN2 back to Calais.

Jacquet would not return to the front lines for nearly a year, most likely given a well-needed, but forced recuperation: he had been flying on the front lines since the beginning of the war!

When the Belgian AIr Force decided to follow the French Air Service's example and finally organized their fighter units into a Group de Chasse in March 1918, Jacquet was brought back as its commander by direct insistence of King Albert himself.

By this time, the Germans had put more air assets opposite the Belgians, Jagdgruppe Dixmuiden was composed of Jastas 7, 29, 33 and 35b. Jacquet's old pusher aircraft were now hopelessly outclassed and although Jacquet fought for the Bristol F2b fighter, he was assigned a Spad XI since this aircraft type was already being used by the Belgians.

He also needed a new observer/gunner and for the remainder of the war teamed up with Lt. Marcel de Cromrugge de Looringhe.

In the mess for the new fighter group, Jacquet shared a table with fellow aces Coppens and Olieslagers. No doubt this helped to plan the sortie on the 5th June 1918 when Jacquet flew as an escort as Coppens scored his 6th victory by burning a balloon over the Houthulst Forest. During this action Jacquet forced down a German Fokker triplane by shooting up its rudder and tailplane which required the German pilot into a forced landing. The Fokker triplane was leading the German kette and likely flown by the German ace Josef Jacobs.

Jacquet and de Cromrugge encountered Jacobs once again on 2nd October. Jacobs was again flying his Fokker triplane while leading more than 10 Fokker DVIIs distributed in several flights. The German fighters were escorting an observation plane , which was directly attacked by the Belgians despite the escorting fighters. Jacquet was unable to down the two-seater but drove it away and disrupted its mission.

Jacquet and de Cromrugge were then set upon by the Germans, whom they successfully fought off. However, Jacobs put in for and was credited his 36th victory, stating he had downed a two-seater Spad just NE of Houthulst Forest. Jacquet and de Cromrugge made it safely back to their base.

Therefore, it seems that Jacquet and Jacobs each "downed" each other, although only Jacobs was given formal credit. Jacquet and de Cromrugge would score two confirmed victories while flying together with their last victory coming on 6th November 1918. It was Jacquet's 7th confirmed victory, and the

Above: Belgian Spad 11 with crew.

Right: Belgian Spad 11 in flight, believed to be King Albert I in the back cockpit.

last victory of the war for the Av.M.

Captain-Commander Fernand Jacquet, the nearsighted ace, had thus accomplished:

The first official victory of the war for the Av.M.

He was the first Belgian ace of the war

He scored the last official victory of the war for the Av.M.

Having flown from the start of the war in August 1914, he was still flying front line combat missions at the end of the war in November 1918: he would fly a total of 598 combat sorties, making him the most active pilot for the Av.M. in the war and in the end, he was involved in 126 air combats.

It is quite clear, that It was not simply because of his defective vision that made Jacquet a memorable fighter ace and a hero for his country: but his unwavering courage and dedication to his duty from the start to the end of the war.

Above: Josef Jacobs in front of his Fokker Triplane, an aircraft he continued to prefer even after the introduction of the Fokker DVII. Jacobs scored 48 victories and was awarded the Pour le Mérite.

Above: Jacobs' distinct all-black Fokker Triplane that he flew while commander of Jasta 7. Jacobs's triplane had a French Clerget rotary engine salvaged from a downed Allied aircraft.

Above: From L to R: Jean Olieslagers, Abel De Neef, Robin, Jacquet, Prince Jean de Caraman.

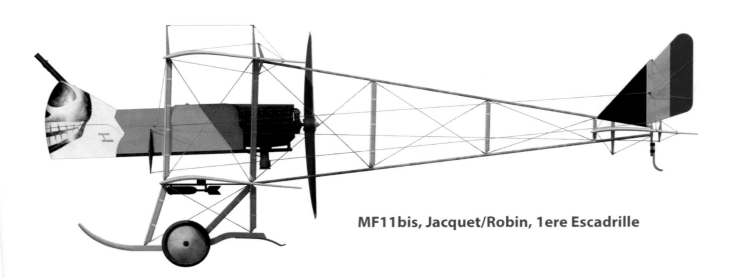

MF11bis, Jacquet/Robin, 1ere Escadrille

Big Birds

Above: The Sikorsky Il'ya Muromets was a large aircraft; note the inline engines on this aircraft, EVK Warsaw 1915. It was by far the most successful Russian-designed and built aircraft of the war.

When most aviation or military historians think of First World War aviation their thoughts and efforts seem to rapidly focus on fighter aces, their aircraft and their deeds. However, their combined contributions would only be minimal in the overall scope of the war. Another aspect of military aviation that saw its development in the war was that of bombing: both tactical and strategic.

The success of the bomber in World War One has been debated over the years and it is not unusual to read conclusions that downplay the overall significance of the bomber in the war: too few total aircraft, very limited useful bomb load, limited range, etc. All reasonable points and in fact, the bombers used in WWI were of limited significance.

However, the Wright brothers' first successful flight was in December,1903. The flight covered 120 feet and lasted 12 seconds. Six years later Bleroit flew across the English Channel, covering the 22 miles in about 36 minutes. Only nine years later, the R.A.F. had seven squadrons of Handley Page 0/400 bombers capable of eight hours of flight, a ceiling of 8,000 feet, a maximum speed of 90 mph and were each capable of carrying over 1,500 pound of bombs.

The development of large aircraft during the First World War set the stage for the development of the first civilian airliners, transport aircraft, and aircraft capable of long flights that would, post war, establish air routes that are used even today by commercial airlines. Therefore the capabilities developed in the big birds of WWI were arguably more crucial to the development of the commercial aviation industry than the small fighter aircraft, so often lionized in the numerous books already written about first world war aviation.

There were also clear examples of successes during the war as the military commanders of the combatants learned how to use this new weapon of war.

The most advanced big bird at the start of the war was without doubt the four engined Il'ya Muromets designed by Igor Sikorsky. The aircraft design was introduced by the brilliant Sikorsky in 1913 and at that time was known as The Grand. It was the world's first four-engined aircraft and was capable of an unheard of 400 mile range. The aircraft set distance records and records for carrying the most passengers.In February 1914 the very first Il'ya Muromets carried 16 people to an altitude of 2,000 meters. It had salon seating and even a balcony to stand in to watch the earth pass below!

The lack of Russian aviation manufacturing capabilities would limit the number of these impressive aircraft that saw service in the war and

Илья Муромецъ.

Above: This example has rotary engines which tended to give poorer performance overall; a shortage of engines compelled the Russian Air Service to use what they had on their big bird.

Below: The Il'ya Muromets' performance allowed it to carry some very large bombs. Designer Igor Sikorski is the young civilian man second to left of the large bomb in the front row.

Above: The vast expanse of the Eastern Front was not an overwhelming deterrent to the capabilities of the Il'ya Muromet, which could be used for strategic bombing of significant targets located well behind the front lines. John Richards.

Below: The first four-engined aircraft, designed before the war began, served with distinction within the Russian Air Service in a multitude of roles. Shigeo Koike.

Above: A more typical bomb load in the process of being loaded; note the upper wing gunner. The aircraft normally could carry from 1,000 to 2,200 pounds of bombs depending on overall distance that needed to be flown to the target.

Below: A combat photo of an Il'ya Muromets flying through extensive AA fire to its target.

Above: The French relied on building numbers of medium sized bombers for their strategy of emphasizing tactical bombing in WWI; here is the very capable Breguet 14 in flight from an American bombing squadron. Fast, with a metal airframe, the Breguet was the best day-bomber of the war.

an even bigger factor in limiting their contributions was the severe shortage of aircraft engines. Multiple combinations of different engines, both rotary and in-line types of various horsepower were utilized. This fact led to very different performance capabilities in the individual aircraft.

However, every Il'ya Muromets was capable of long distance flight and could carry multiple cameras so that an individual aircraft, during a single sortie could take enough photos to document the entire front lines in various locations along the Eastern Front. The aircraft could also absorb a lot of punishment during these missions, one aircraft was found to have been hit over 100 times and still completed its mission without difficulty.

When used as a bomber, the aircraft carried between 5 to 7 crew, with three to four machine guns for defense and a bomb load capacity of over 1,000 pounds! In fact, only one Il'ya Muromets was shot down during the war, despite the types usage on every front and during every battle in which the Russian Army was involved.

The large distances that were typical of the warfare on the Eastern Front posed no challenge to the Il'ya Muromets. The aircraft were eventually organized into the Escadra Vozdushnykh Korablei (EVK) or squadron of flying ships. Their missions were primarily reconnaissance and strategic bombing. In the bombing role the EVK aircraft would hit targets such as vital railway hubs, supply depots, airfields and even were known to attack German divisional headquarters.

A pilot who would earn multiple medals as an EVK pilot, Jezups Bashko flew the first EVK mission in February 1915. He would fly to the end of the war and would fly the most missions, 81 and log 229 combat hours in his aircraft. A mission that reveals both the skills and courage of Bashko and the reliability of Sikorsky's design occurred on 19 July 1915.

To maximize the bomb load, only a single light machine gun and a rifle were brought on the mission. Bashko guided his aircraft to over 25 miles behind enemy lines and bombed two airfields and two separate railway stations.

It was then that three German two-seater LVG aircraft engaged the Russian behemoth and in their first pass caused damage to the fuel lines to both of

Above: Not building their own "big bird", the French Air Service instead built thousands of Breguet 14 aircraft, a very sound design capable of tactical bombing. On 5th February 1918 several American aviators were sent to a French bombing escadrille (Br. 123) to gain combat experience. One of them was Stephen W. Thompson ,who managed to shoot down an attacking German fighter. His victory was the first ever for a USAS trained airman, but it was not recognized or given its official status until 1967. Michael O'Neal.

the left engines causing them both to stop. On their second pass the Germans wounded Bahsko in both his head and leg, forcing him to give up the controls to his co-pilot Smirnov.

Also, the fuel filter to the right side engines had been damaged and one of the crew had to cover the hole in the fuel filter with their bare hand in order to keep the right side engines functioning. Two crew members took turns as the altitude quickly caused their hands to go numb from the cold.

Bashko had by this time re-taken the flight controls and was guiding the stricken aircraft back towards the Russian lines. Another German aircraft approached to attack the giant bomber as it was descending to a height of 4,000 feet. Fortunately for the Russian aviators, some shots from their rifle were enough to dissuade the German from pressing his attack. As the aircraft passed over the Russian trenches at only 2,000 feet both of the right engines now stopped.

A "dead stick" landing had never been attempted before in an Il'ya Muromets and was actually thought to be impossible. Bashko chose a field and successfully landed his aircraft. The airframe was judged irreparable but all the Russian aviators survived!

In September 1917 Bashko flew his bomber on a non-stop flight of 7.5 hours! At times, the EVK unit would co-ordinate all out efforts with fighter units. One such mission saw seven bombers being escorted by 26 fighters: which brings to mind similar such missions that would be performed quite regularly in WWII.

On 26 April 1916 Lt. A.M. Konstenchik lead several bombers from IM-10 to bomb the key railway depot at Davdzevas. This key supply station had been attacked before and so had a significant number of anti-aircraft guns to protect it. Despite that fact and despite being wounded by shrapnel during his bombing run, Kostenchik and his flight managed to

Above: The Gotha bomber carried an external bomb load and had front/rear gunners for protection. This G.V is in dark camouflage for night bombing.

Below: The England Gesschwader was a special unit designated to carry out attacks against the English homeland with the hope of undermining the morale of its citizens.

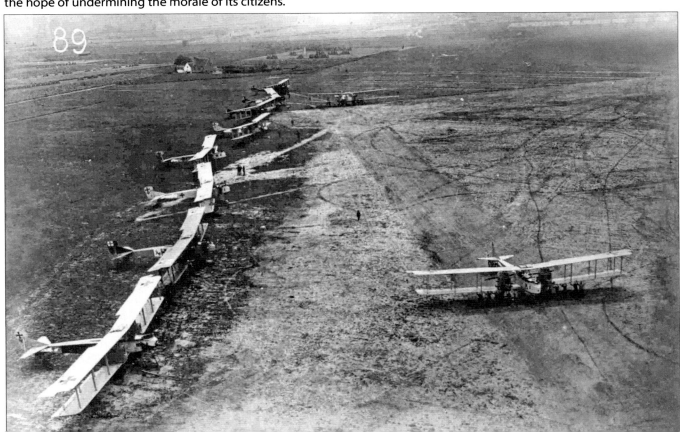

Above: Only two raids actually reached London; this is a photo of one of those missions as the Gothas were photographed from somewhere in the English capital below the German bombers.

hit an ammunition train that was in the depot and completely destroyed his target.

This is just one example of the successes enjoyed by the aircrews of Sikorsky's brilliant design. The EVK would fly over 400 missions during the war and drop more than 44,000 pounds of bombs on enemy targets.

While the Russians could boast of having the most advanced design for a bomber at the start of the war the French could boast of being the farthest

along in the deployment and strategic use of its bombers. Unfortunately for the French their Voison pusher aircraft were slow and could carry only very small bomb loads. This did not prevent the French from forming the first Groupe de Bombardement G.B.1 in November, 1914. The group flew its first daylight strategic bombing mission into Germany on 4th December 1914. On the 26th May 1915, the group flew a five hour mission to bomb the poison gas factories located at Ludwigshafen. This group

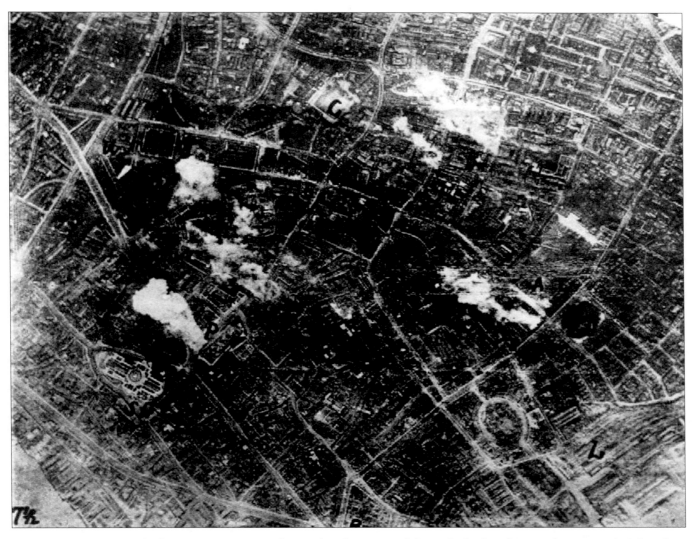

Above: At approximately the same moment, a photo taken from one of those Gotha bombers to document their bomb strikes on London.

would perform tactical attacks against gun batteries, railway stations, airfields and other targets located some distances behind the front lines. The group also would try to mount strategic missions against targets in nearby Germany when possible. Soon however, the French could no longer attack targets in daylight as there were no escorting fighters and most of the valuable targets now had defensive fighter squadrons and increasingly better anti-aircraft defenses.

In November, 1917 the French introduced a two-seater bomber, the Breguet 14 B2. It was a very good aircraft, but had a duration of only 2hours and 30 minutes and a bomb load of just over 500 pounds.

Still, by the end of the war the French could send formations of 60-100 Breguet aircraft escorted by Spad fighters to strike at targets behind the front lines. Although the French never developed

their own "big bird" aircraft type, they saw the importance of bombing. Between 1917 and 1918, the French doubled the number of bombardment groups from 5 to 10 and as a result they increased the total weight of bombs dropped, primarily on tactical targets, 18 fold!

It is likely that the most well-known big bird from the First World War is the German Gotha bomber. Its notoriety in history likely derived from its use in attacks over Britain and especially in the bombing raids on London. Several versions of the Gotha bomber were produced, but an average of the types' performances would give the G.IV a range of just over 300 miles, and a bomb load of just over 1000 pounds. In order to make an attack on London, the aircraft had to be modified for the distance and could only carry six, 110 pound bombs that had to be carried externally.

Above: A Gotha G.IV bomber in flight.

The image of Gotha bombers flying at will over English soil raining bombs down upon innocent civilians is a potent and enduring image of the First World War. However, the facts force a significant re-write into this storyline.

As the Zeppelin attacks proved to be too costly in lost airships, the thrust of the German campaign against England in the hope of bringing the civilian population to its knees and ask for peace fell to the Gotha equipped bombing units. Thus, in the early summer of 1917 the aircraft campaign was begun:

- 25 May- 21 Gothas, with clouds noted over London, turned to Folkestone and dropped their bombs there, not a single British plane intercepted the German bombers
- 5 June- 22 Gothas, again bad weather forced them to turn away from London and the bombers attacked several locations, before re-grouping for their flight back to base
- 13 June- 18 of 20 Gotha bombers reached and

Above: On the 7th July, German Gotha bombers bombed London for the second time. This time, there were British fighters that managed to intercept the intruders. Note that St. Paul's cathedral is visible amongst the smoke below, a sight that will be noted again in the Summer of 1940. Mark Postlethwaite

Below: A Zeppelin-Staaken Giant, R.IV. Wingspans of these aircraft were generally twice that of Gotha bombers. On some missions one or two of these aircraft would accompany more numerous Gothas on night missions over England.

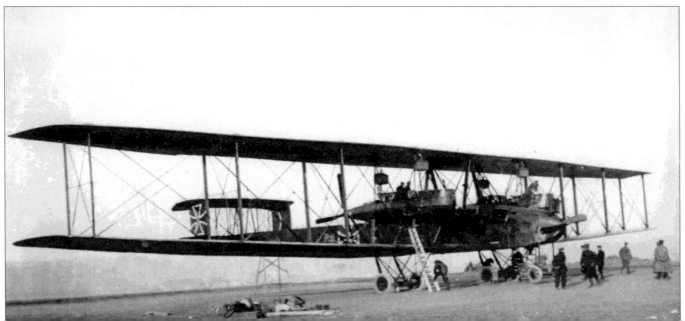

Above: The river Thames unfortunately provided an easy navigational tool for German bombers to find London. Brian Knight

bombed London for the first time, still not a single British plane took off to intercept them.

- 7 July- 21 Gotha bombers reached London, dispersed over the city and bombed at will,

then re-grouped to fly home. 30 British interceptors made contact, one Gotha shot down and two British fighters were lost.

- 22 August- the last of only nine daylight raids over England during the war, only two

Above: Very quickly the German bombers had to revert to night time missions because of the inherent risks of a vigorous daytime response from the British defensive units. Steve Anderson

of which actually reached London.

By August of 1917, the defenses around London were such that the German bombing force could no longer fly daylight missions without the risk of significant losses. The impact of the Gotha attacks were several:
1. Several British fighter squadrons were withdrawn from the Western Front and so diminished the effective fighter force there
2. Although not in the least bit cowered, the response from the British people led the government to allocate resources to mount a bombing campaign against strategic targets in Germany. Part of this response would lead to the formation of the Independent Force (IF).
3. The development of a fully functional and robust defense system of London, which was the start of what would become a vastly expanded and modern defense system that would ultimately lead to a successful outcome in the Battle of

Britain in the summer of 1940.

Beginning in September 1917 and until the last mission of 19/20 May 1918 German Gothas would periodically still bomb targets in England at night. The ability to actually hit the intended target was nearly impossible at this time during night flight. The Gotha bombers were joined on 19 nighttime bombing raids by one or two Giant bombers. The Giants were manufactured by several different aircraft companies but were all very similar in their enormous size with their wingspans being twice that of the Gotha bombers. Each Giant could carry 3,500 pounds of bombs on its mission!

Gotha bombers ultimately proved to be inadequate to the task of being a successful strategic bomber. They were quite capable of tactical bombing and would be utilized in that role during much of the war. The German High Command failed to take these lessons into the next war and never developed a functional strategic bomber, which also

Above: German giant aircraft were first deployed on the Eastern Front in August, 1916 to counter the success of the Il'ya Muromets. One of the two units, Rfa.501, under the command of Capt. Richard von Bentivegni, was sent to Belgium to complement the ongoing Gotha raids. R.39 was the aircraft that von Bentivegni personally used during the bombing raids against England. He was not a pilot, he would function as the aircraft commander, navigator and bombadier. On the evening of 28th January 1918, after having just shot down a Bristol Fighter, R.39 struck a balloon cable apron on its way towards London. The concept of the balloon cables surrounding London was multiple steel cables were "hung" from other cables that stretched from one balloon to another balloon. The balloons would be flown at a designated height and would thus force them to fly over the steel cable apron and give a more accurate altitude for anti-aircraft guns to shoot at. As a result of the collision, R.39 tore two cables loose and was able to continue on its bomb run to London, where it dropped 2,000 lbs. of bombs and R.39 would successfully return to its base. Staaken R.12 shown here above London also struck a balloon cable 16/17 Feb. 1918 and went on the bomb London. R.12 was the only Giant bomber that served on both the Eastern and Western Fronts. Robert Karr

Facing Page, Below: In contrast to the German Gothas and Giants, initially the British strategic bombing force, the IF, was equipped with the DH 4 which was capable of only a modest payload of bombs and proved to be vulnerable to the concerted efforts of German fighter units flying in defense against the IF's missions. The DH 9 was also used by the IF; the DH 9 used the DH 4 airframe powered by an unreliable, under-powered engine that gave poor performance and made it exceptionally vulnerable to the German fighters. Roy Cross

Although this photo is actually of DH 9a aircraft on a training mission after the war, it illustrates how an Independent Force mission of DH 4 or DH 9 aircraft would have appeared during the war. The wooden structure of the DH 9a was more dangerous to the crew in event of a crash than the metal frame of the Breguet 14 B2, regulating it to the second best day bomber of the war.

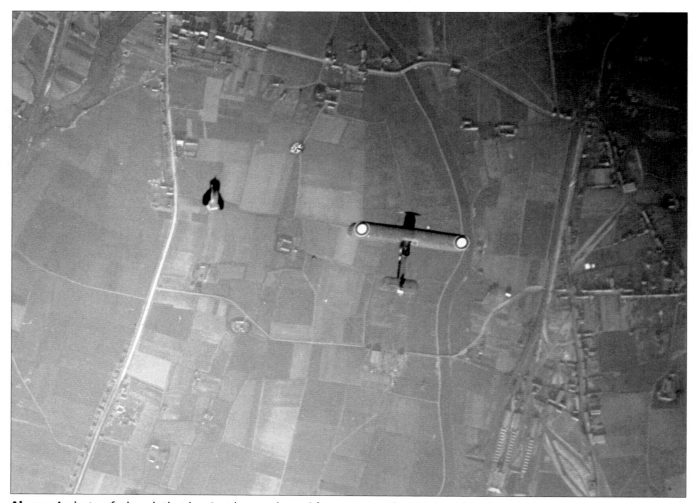

Above: A photo of a bomb that has just been released from an aircraft at higher altitude as it drops past a DH 4 from the same formation of bombers.

Below: This photo of a single DH 9a flying over Mannheim gives an indication of why the IF was not successful until the advent of its own big bird, too few aircraft, scattered formations, and minimal bombloads to impact any single target of value.

Above: A good representation of a flight of IF DH 4 bombers on their way to a target. They did not have any escorting fighter aircraft because of the distances involved to their strategic targets and thus had to depend on their gunners for protection: often the flights would be decimated either on the way to or from the target. Brian Knight

contributed to their losing the Battle of Britain in 1940.

Quite differently from the Germans, the British put significant faith and resources into developing a strategic bomber force. There was a concerted effort by the British government to impress the public and to improve its morale by embarking on a strategic bombing campaign that would retaliate against targets in Germany for the bombing of civilians in England. Coupled with the fact that the French bombing units had effectively stopped any large

scale efforts against strategic targets in Germany (except for continued small scale night time sorties), an independent force was formed in October 1917. Major General Hugh Trenchard was put in command of this unit whose identification changed several times during the conflict:

- No.41 wing- October 1917
- VIII Brigade, RFC- February 1918
- Independent Force (IF), RAF- June 1918.

For simplicity sake, the unit will be called IF here throughout. Initially the IF was composed of

Above: With the advent of the Handley Page "Bloody Paralyzer", the Independent Force could begin to have an impact on strategic targets.

Facing Page, Above: The enormous size of the Handley Page is apparent as this example comes in to land

Facing Page, Below: A Handley Page 0/400 in flight.

Above: With the introduction of the Handley Page 0/100 and 0/400 aircraft, the IF could at last strike their strategic targets with achievable results and with less concern towards German defensive fighter attacks. Merv Corning

four squadrons of DH 4 and DH 9 bombers. Two-seater aircraft with reasonable performances, their main drawback was slow speed (compared to the German defensive fighter aircraft) and bomb load capacity of 400-450 pounds: less bombs could be carried if the target was farther away. Thus, at first, Trenchard was faced with a very difficult choice.

Use his aircraft on tactical targets closer to the front lines, for which the designs were more suitable. Or use the aircraft on strategic targets in Germany for what would have to be termed propaganda purposes.

The IF units suffered great losses as they attempted to perform strategic bombing roles during daylight. The typical IF formation of aircraft would

Above: The Handley Page bombers were primarily used on night missions. An advanced version to the British "Big Bird", capable of reaching Berlin was just being deployed to the front lines as the Armistice ended hostilities. Steve Anderson

be attacked by frontline German fighter units as they headed towards their targets. The speed with which they would approach the intended target was such that as they crossed the front lines, the German defenses were usually alerted and waiting for them at the target. After fighting their way over the target, the IF formations would then be forced to contend once again with front line German units who had re-fueled and re-armed in the meantime.

Two examples from 99 Squadron provide clarification on the potentially devastating odds facing the British airmen on every mission:

- 31st July 1918: target railway station at Mainz, 12 aircraft took off, 3 had to return for various problems before reaching the target, 7 of the remaining 9 aircraft were shot down
- 26th September: target railway station at

Thionville, 10 aircraft took off, 3 had to return to base before the target, 6 of the remaining 7 aircraft were shot down and the only aircraft to make it back to base did so with the observer having been killed during the air combat

The courage exhibited by the British airmen in the daylight bombing units of the IF cannot be over-estimated.

Remember that Trenchard, as leader of the RFC, had experienced Bloody April. Yet, his personal secretary Maurice Baring wrote this:

"Of all the experiences we[Trenchard/Baring] had in connection with aviation, there was none more trying, more harassing, and more hard to bear for those who were responsible than waiting for these long distance raids to return. The distances were so great...the margin of safety was so narrow, the

Above: The Caproni bomber in flight. A tri-motor design, it was capable of flight with only one of its three engines.

Above: The pilot and co-pilot literally sat in front of the two large fuel tanks in the Caproni design.

Above: A Caproni bomber in a Rome Air Museum. Note the elaborate "cage" for the rear gunner to climb to the top for a defensive capability to protect the rear of the aircraft; this cage protected the gunner from the center propeller.

Right: The most famous Caproni crew of the First World War, Gori (L) and Pagliano (R). Note the list of their missions prominently displayed on their aircraft, a practice that many bomber crews in WW II would continue.

Above: By the end of the war, the Italian air Service could mount raids of numerous Caproni bombers that were fully escorted by fighter aircraft to and from their targets. Bill Marsalko

determination on the part of the pilots to attempt all that there was to be attempted was so certain, that whenever one knew there was a big and long raid on one could not help being desperately uneasy till the machines had come back. It was not merely a question of losing one or two machines...one might easily lose the whole formation."

The IF also had night bombing units, which at first utilized the F.e. 2 aircraft. These sorties must be thought more of as nuisance raids because of the few numbers of total aircraft, the profound difficulty in accurately bombing a specific target at night and the compromised bomb load that could be carried.

However, the argument could be made that the IF forced the Germans to deploy fighter aircraft, and anti-aircraft guns to protect these targets and thus were denied their use on the Western Front. Also, the Germans had far fewer overall resources available to them and so every unit pulled from the front lines was probably even more critical than had been the diverted Allied units to respond to the German bombing efforts.

The British finally found their successful big bird when the Handley Page 0/100 began operations in September 1916. It had a 100 foot wingspan, it could cruise at approximately 75-80 mph ,it had a range of nearly 700 miles and could carry a maximum bomb load of 2,000 pounds (5x the load carried by a DH 4). It would be replaced by the even more powerful 0/400 aircraft which would be nicknamed "The Bloody Paralyzer".

Initially used as a day bomber, the Handley Pages were quickly changed over to a night bomber with tactics that would be repeated in WWII by Bomber Command. On the evening of 14/15th September 40 Handley Page 0/400 bombers ranged over the SAAR region of Germany, each with 1,700 pounds of bombs.

Remember that the Handley Page bombers were open cockpit aircraft, one pilot wrote:

"The worst part when flying in the open cockpit of an HP was keeping warm and dry. At night, with freezing temperatures, rain, sleet, snow, darkness, often in cloud, drifting fog, no breaks, no connection with the ground, it did not make for happiness."

Just over 30 years later, RAF Lancasters would be flying through the same night skies and bombing the same targets.

Above: One of the most significant targets of the Caproni bombers during the war were the Austro-Hungarian naval bases at Pola and Trieste. German submarines operating in the Mediterranean Sea relied on these bases for re-fitting after a mission; by disrupting these bases as resources for the U-boats, the Italian bombers made a significant contribution to the Allied efforts in the naval war of this region. Merv Corning

The Handley Page bomber started to prove that with the proper aircraft, strategic bombing could be successful in its mission. A version of the "Bloody Paralyzer" was being readied to have the range to strike Berlin, but the war ended before it could be deployed.

However, arguable the most successful bomber aircraft and the most successful strategic bombing campaign of the First World War was the efforts of the Italian Air Force and their Caproni Ca 3. It was a three-engined aircraft that could be flown even with only one of its engines functioning. The Ca.3 had a

Courtesy Berto Rutkowski

Above: In response to the Allied strategic bombing campaign, German air units were formed as defensive squadrons to protect targets in Germany. Initially they were supplied with "retired" front-line fighter aircraft. Here Kampfeinsitzerstaffel (Kest) 4b was photographed after they moved from Böblingen to Freiburg im Breisgau on 15 April 1917. One Fokker E.IV is seen at left; a Halberstadt fighter is in the background with Fokker D.II and D.III fighters filling out the roster.

Above: German aircraft designers specifically developed an aircraft capable of flying as an interceptor aircraft in order to protect crucial strategic targets in Germany. The best of these designs, the SSW D.III & D.IV, would prove to be very effective in that role. A flight of Kest 5 aircraft is shown. Steve Anderson

duration of 3.5 hours and could carry 1,000 pounds of bombs. In addition, its multi-wheeled landing gear could function from rough fields quite well.

The Caproni bombers would be used throughout the war to attack the Austro-Hungarian naval bases of Trieste and Pola. German submarines attempting to prowl the Mediterranean Sea used these Adriatic Sea bases to refit and re-supply. The Italians were able to significantly hinder those activities throughout the war and also keep the Austro-Hungarian naval units checked by their frequent bombing missions.

The first raid over Trieste was carried out by 22 Caproni bombers in September 1916. In comparison,

the first Gotha bombing raid was not until June 1917. By that time the Caproni units had completed 540 bombing missions and were now flying in formations of 30 bombers. By the end of the war, staggered formations of 100 bombers being escorted to and from the target by fighter aircraft were not unusual. By the end of the war, there would be 15 bombing squadrons deployed.

It did help that the overall distances needed to be flown by the Italian bombers were much less than those on the Western Front. In terms of overall impact during the First World War, it is likely the efforts of the Italian Caproni bombers during the Battle of Vittorio Veneto would have to be ranked at

Facing Page, Below: The Siemens-Schuckert D.III was an innovative design tailored to be an interceptor so as to better protect strategic targets in Germany. The aircraft used a counter-rotary engine in which the engine spun in an opposite direction from the propeller. This design allowed the use of a larger, more efficient propeller which gave the type an exceptional climb rate and good speed to catch Allied bombers.

the top.

The battle lasted from 24 October until the 3rd November 1918. At the end of the battle, the Allies took approximately 450,000 prisoners: including 100,000 German troops fighting with their Austro-Hungarian compatriots. The range of even the most effective artillery piece at the time was about 14 miles. However, just over 20 miles behind the battle lines were key bridges over several rivers and key railroad junctions that could bring supplies and reinforcements. It was these strategic targets that the Italian bombers struck again and again. Day after day, any repaired bridge was once again destroyed and any train found blown apart.

It was also very likely, that the German and Austro-Hungarian troops knew there was no retreat for them since they were trapped between the mountains and the Adriatic Sea and now they could not retreat over the rivers or be withdrawn by rail. With the collapse of these army units, the Austro-Hungarian government sued for peace and an armistice was signed 24 hours later.

Part of that armistice was that the Allied military units could immediately travel freely throughout the Austro-Hungarian Empire.

This meant that very quickly the Allies could position themselves on the southern border of Germany and open another front. This likely was a significant factor in leading to Germany quickly requesting its own armistice on November 11th.

The dominoes that fell, could be in part traced back to the sustained and successful efforts of the Italian Caproni crews: an unqualified success of strategic bombing.

No 134   30th Anniversary Issue   Nov 1991
W·W·1
Aero
THE JOURNAL OF THE EARLY AEROPLANE

Above: The Germans were developing a transatlantic bomber to attack New York City. The Poll Giant never got very far in development; artist Keith Woodcock shows a possible appearance as two of the bombers circle NYC. Courtesy of Leo Opdycke.

Dragon Master Of Tsingtau

It did not take long for the First World War to develop into its world wide encompassing scope, far-flung colonial outposts of the European powers were quickly brought into the fray. Germany had established a small city and naval base at Tsingtao [now Qingdao], China.

Germany had wanted to project an element of naval power into Asia and therefore established the East Asia Squadron, to be based at Tsingtao, China. Naturally, Great Britain did not exactly welcome this action and in 1902 signed an alliance with Japan in the hope of securing a formidable ally to help quash any German threat in the Pacific.

With the outbreak of war, there was little hesitation when Japan declared war upon Germany on 23rd August 1914 and then immediately sent an ultimatum for the Germans to relinquish Tsingtau and to transfer the city into Japanese control. The Germans predictably ignored the ultimatum and the Siege of Tsingtau would soon began, lasting from 31st October until the 7th November, representing the only battle fought in the far east during the First World War.

Although the British sent some supporting troops, the battle was primarily a Japanese effort with 20,000 troops and 140 artillery pieces making the outcome a foregone conclusion. This relatively small scale battle would produce several aviation historical firsts.

Among the ships of the IJN was the seaplane carrier *Wakamiya* with four Maurice Farman seaplanes. These sea planes would provide valuable reconnaissance of the German defenses and would also be involved in the first known air-sea battle when on the 6th September they bombed the Austrian cruiser *Kaisern Elisabeth*, without success. These sea planes also participated in the first night bombing raid on the 28th October during a full moon.

On the 30th September the *Wakamiya* had hit a mine and had to be beached, However the Japanese established a seaplane base on a beach at LaoShan harbor and continued their air offensive unabated. The naval aircraft were also eventually joined by a contingent of Army Maurice Farmans as well, with the result that the German defenders of Tsingtao were under fairly constant surveillance as well as being bombed on a regular basis.

The aircraft were able to direct the fire from both naval guns and army artillery units quite effectively and would lead to the destruction of German defensive artillery positions, severely inhibiting the

Above: Gunther Pluschow- the dragon master of Tsingtao in the cockpit of his Taube.

Germans from defending Tsingtao.

The Germans also had aircraft involved in the battle, and they also had a very charismatic aviator: Gunther Pluschow. Pluschow was a graduate of several highly esteemed military academies and had chosen a career in the German Navy. He was assigned to the SMS *Furst Bismarck*, the flagship of the German East Asia Squadron based at Tsingtau from 1907-1910. During this deployment, Pluschow acquired an elaborate tattoo, a multi-hued dragon whose tail began on Pluschow's left shoulder and the dragon then extended down the length of his left arm until its head was upon the left fore-arm.

At the end of this Asian adventure, Pluschow then returned to Germany and after several more assignments, Pluschow was able to gain a transfer to the naval aviation corp (with the help of an influential uncle).

He reported to Johannistahl airfield outside of Berlin for pilot training in January 1914. It seems he was a natural pilot and swiftly progressed through training. Pluschow was elated when he learned that

Above: Just before the start of WWI, and only three days after Lt. Freidrich Muellerskowski completely destroyed one of two Taube aircraft in a crash, Pluschow suffered an engine failure and made a forced landing.

his new posting as a fledgling naval pilot would bring him back to Tsingtau!

Thus, navy Lt. Pluschow found himself back in his beloved Tsingtau in June of 1914. Joining him was another naval pilot, Lt. Friedreich Muellerskowski. They were informed that two Rumpler Taube aircraft were to be delivered in July in order to establish the aviation unit at Tsingtao. On the 26th July 1914 Lt. Pluschow made the first flight with one of the taubes, and was given the title of Lung Gong Tau (dragon master because of his tattoo).

Unfortunately, on the 31st July Lt. Muellerskowski crashed the second Rumpler Taube from a height of approximately 50 meters which resulted in the aircraft being destroyed and the pilot with multiple fractures. From that moment onwards, the entire German Air Force in the far east consisted of Pluschow and his taube.

With the beginning of the war, Pluschow would fly as often as possible and perform critical reconnaissance for the Tsingtao garrison. With the arrival of the Japanese forces, Pluschow and his aircraft became prime targets so that the Germans would not have the ability to observe the Allied troop movements or the location of Allied ships.

Pluschow flew from a very small, narrow improvised airfield that was originally an equestrian racecourse at Iltis Platz. He would have to fly in tight spirals from a high altitude in order to land, because as soon as his aircraft was spotted Allied artillery units would fire upon the landing spot: it was unusual for Pluschow to not have to land under direct fire.

Also, the Japanese aircraft would frequently bomb the Iltis Platz which necessitated having a group of Chinese laborers always available to fill in any bomb or shell craters. On one occasion Pluschow was attacked in the air by a Japanese aircraft dropping several of its bombs at him from a

Right: A contemporary journal shows Pluschow's Taube above the town.

Plüschow über Tsingtau

Heft 34   Kolonial-Bücherei   20 Pf.

higher altitude.

Pluschow had been ordered to not engage the Japanese aircraft because the German commanders did not want to risk their only ability at reconnaissance of the Allied forces.

Yet, on 28th September 1914 Lt. Pluschow states that he attacked a formation of the Japanese naval aircraft en route to bomb Tsingtau. He approached until very close to one of the Maurice Farman biplanes and fired 30 rounds from his 9mm Parabellum mauser. Records indicate that a Japanese naval aviator, Lt. Shigematsu, was KIA around this time but it was not recorded in what manner Lt. Shigematsu was killed.

Therefore, aviation historians are skeptical of the claim, especially since Pluschow did not report his success immediately and did not officially request confirmation from his superiors. However, it has been argued that Pluschow would not have done so since he was flagrantly disobeying orders by

Above: After his escape before the surrender of German forces, Pluschow flew to Haichow where he was forced to finally land his aircraft just outside the city walls. He would "present" the Mercedes engine to the local Magistrate as a bargaining chip for assistance to carry on in his escape to Germany.

Facing Page, Above: The IJN seaplane carrier *Wakamiya* launching one of its Maurice Farman floatplanes, the Japanese naval airmen managed several "firsts" for military aviation during the siege of Tsingtao.

Facing Page, Below: After striking a mine, the *Wakamiya* was forced to beach itself, and a seaplane base was established in LaoShan harbor.

Right: After his return to Germany, Pluschow was promoted and awarded several honors for his incredible efforts during the siege, as well as his ability to make it back to Germany.

Kapitänleutnant Plüschow, der Flieger von Tsingtau.

Above: On 26th September 1914 Pluschow stated that he managed do shoot down a Japanese Maurice Faman bomber from a formation attacking Tsingtao, this would be the first successful example of an air-to-air combat by an armed combatant in history. Some military aviation historians doubt the veracity of this claim. Russell Smith

attacking the Japanese formation.

If he did accomplish an aerial victory at this time, it would have been the first successful victory in air to air combat of the war!

Regardless, the German garrison at Tsingtau was doomed. On 6th November 1914, Lt. Pluschow took off in his Rumpler Taube bearing the last dispatches and letters from the German administration and remaining citizens. He flew nearly 250 kilometers until landing at Hainchow. There he presented the engine to the local mandarin and burned his aircraft.

From there he embarked on a remarkable journey which lead him to the United States, which he crossed. Then he sailed on a ship that was bound for Italy, however bad weather forced the ship into the harbor at Gibraltar where Pluschow was captured.

He was sent to a POW camp in Donington, Hall, Leicestershire; from which he escaped and after making his way to Holland, he eventually returned to a hero's welcome in Germany!

He is the only German POW , in either world war, to successfully escape from England. He was promoted, decorated and placed in charge of the naval base at Libau in Latvia for the remainder of the war. After the war Pluschow would lead a life of adventure and exploration in South America until he was killed in January 1931 while flying his floatplane in Argentina.

Unsung Heroes

Above: A photo displaying grim humor, does reveal that the aviators who performed the yeoman work of the air services in the First World War, the two-seater crews, knew the dangers they faced.

"Up above I am a mark for the gunners. But I am a free bird that does not need to crouch motionless. I can employ the circles of a hunted animal to wriggle my way through the narrow meshes of the net of steel splinters and leaden bullets that is set for me."

Hauptman Heydemarck

If someone were to judge who were the heroes of aviation in the First World War solely based on the number of books written, the inevitable conclusion would be the successful fighter pilots, the aces, were those heroes.

From the very beginning, those fighter aces, Guynemer, Ball and Voss among them captured the headlines and the attention of the contemporary press. The belligerent nations utilized these young men to boost morale of both their respective military forces and their civilian populations as well.

Their latest victories were followed and often minutely documented in numerous daily newspapers and special, aviation oriented weekly journals.

After the war's completion, the vast majority of books, journal articles, etc. have continued to focus on those same recognizable fighter aces. Yet, the true overall impact of these pilots to the conduct of military operations was actually quite minimal. In fact, the fighter pilot's greatest importance lay in his ability to thwart the enemy's observation aircraft.

The aviators that did make the most to project "airpower", such as it was in WW I, were the aircrew of the two-seater aircraft that performed the yeoman work of reconnaissance, artillery spotting, photography, ground support and contact patrols(troop coordination). These young men were at the highest risk of danger as they flew over the lines and were the center of attention to the anti-aircraft fire and often were flying at low altitudes which put them in the center of a hailstorm of fire from

Above: A remarkable photo, showing a staged combat which illustrates the preferred method of attack against a two-seater, from behind and below so as to limit the observer's ability to utilize his gun. The leading Italian ace of the war, Francessco Baracca is at the controls of his first victory, Hansa-Brandenbrg C.I 61.57 while his comrade Prince Ruffo di Calabria "attacks" from the right side of the photo.

machine guns and rifles as well.

Although all of the European nations had begun to incorporate aircraft into pre-war army exercises, at the start of the First World War it is safe to say that no air force was considered to be useful by the various high commands and that the military leaders (especially of higher rank) were quite skeptical of the aviators as having any ability to contribute to their execution of a battle.

For good reason, these beliefs changed rather

Above: The team of RNAS aviators in this Nieuport 12 show off their three Lewis guns, undoubtedly a reflection of their intent to do more than "mere"observation during their missions.

Above: At the beginning of the war, observers would occupy the front cockpit and the pilot would sit behind and was considered a chauffeur. The ability of the aircrew to defend themselves from attack are obvious in this painting of an Aviatik aircrew attempt to escape from the attack of a RFC FE 8 fighter. Steve Anderson

quickly once the war began. In addition, a strong argument can be made that the eventual course of the entire First World War was significantly impacted by those tiny air services within the very first weeks of the war.

Mons

On the 22nd of August 1914, French forces began a concentrated and complete re-deployment of their forces from the right flank of the BEF (British Expeditionary Forces). The British had just taken up their positions in a 25-mile sector around the town of Mons. The French did not communicate their changes to the British, who expected them to stay in a position to cover their right flank.

On Saturday, the 22nd, during the course of twelve missions flown that day, airmen reported a large concentration of German forces moving

into position to attack the British. Even more importantly, the airmen documented that the French forces had pulled back to new positions and had exposed the right flank of the BEF.

At first, the reports were dismissed; however, as more and more aircrews returned from their flights with consistent reports, the British commanders in the field began to pay attention. A reconnaissance flight from 3 Sqdn. RFC provided such detail in their report of the French movements that the British High Command pressed for official, written communication from their French counterparts. When they received the written confirmation, the British airmen's reports were vindicated and from that point forward the airmen's stock was on the rise. Their efforts "did much to lift the fog of war".

If not for the virtue of intelligence gained by air reconnaissance, the battle of Mons could have

Above: Seasoned German two-seater crews often flew by themselves, as the fighters were needed in defensive roles and often could not be spared for escort duty. This lead to the aircrews flying at high altitude. The performance capabilities of the German observation aircraft were quite good and made the German aviators confident in their mission capability. Here a crew has fun "taking a self portrait" while on a mission over Allied territory.

Left: German two-seater crews referred to themselves as Franz and Emil: it was not unusual that these "teams" of two airmen would fly almost exclusively together on numerous sorties.

Leutnant Eisenmenger (rechts) und Vfw. Gund, die bei einem Beobachtungsflug von 6 engl. Kampfeinsitzern 4 Flugzeuge abschossen.

636
Postkartenvertrieb W. Sanke
BERLIN N 37.
Nachdruck wird gerichtlich verfolgt

turned out very differently, considering that the coordination between the British and French allies was atrocious.

Perhaps even more importantly, the airmen could keep track of the splintered British forces themselves, so that the retreat could remain orderly and not turn into a rout. The RFC units did much to enable the BEF to remain a cohesive fighting force.

Later, Field Marshal Sir John French wrote of the RFC units during the Battle of Mons:

"I wish particularly to bring to your Lord's notice the admirable work done by the Royal Flying Corps under Sir David Henderson. Their skill, energy and perseverance have been beyond all praise. They have furnished me with the most complete and accurate information which has been of incalculable value in the conduct of operations. Fired at constantly both by friend and foe, and not hesitating to fly in every kind of weather, they have remained undaunted throughout."

Tannenberg

At the very same time, the Russians were following through with a promise they had made to the French before the war. The Russian General Staff had promised their counterparts that they would mount an invasion of East Prussia within two weeks of mobilization. The Russians split their forces into two armies of roughly equal size (each with 300,000 men) and approached East Prussia via a two-pronged attack with the Masurian Lakes between the two armies.

The topography of the land as well as the sheer distances involved during the battle contributed to the importance of the role aviation would play

during the ensuing campaign. Reports via aerial reconnaissance from both airships and aircraft informed the German High Command that the two Russian armies were widely separated and that the southern army under General Samsonov was badly spread out over a sixty mile front.

The much smaller German force split itself based upon this information in order to simultaneously attack both flanks of Samasonov's army group. The German assault was completely successful, inflicting staggering losses upon the Russians, including nearly 90,000 prisoners.

Now the Germans could marshal all of their forces and descend upon the remaining Russian forces to the north. This offensive , the First Battle of the Masurian Lakes, inflicted a further 140,000 casualties upon the Russian forces: who swiftly fled from East Prussia.

This victory was significant in its scope and injury caused to the Russians. More importantly, the scale of victory was such that the Germans still held the upper hand on the Eastern Front and did not have to withdraw troops from the west, keeping the German forces at full strength as they faced the British and French troops. Field Marshal von Hindenburg himself stated:

"Without the airmen–no Tannenberg."

Marne

On the 30th May 1914 General von Kluck ordered the German First Army to continue to move in a south-eastward direction and to maintain contact with the German Second Army. These troop movements were detected and reported upon by the RFC that very same day.

Above: A Hansa-Brandenburg C.I of the Austro-Hungarian Air Service: stable, reliable, and easy to fly, these machines would form the backbone of its observation units. The "baby coffin" on top of the upper wing houses a machine gun for the pilot to use; throughout the war there was a lack of interrupter gear in the Austro-Hungarian Air Service.

Below: Another image of a Hansa-Brandenburg C.I, taking on several bombs for a mission to the front lines. This aircraft would perform numerous mission types throughout the war.

Above: With large ground "spaces" to cover and few aircraft available, the two-seater crews would inevitably function as fighter aircraft if an enemy aircraft was seen. Here an Austro-Hungarian Hansa-Brandenburg battles a Russian Lebed12. Keith Woodcock

Roland-Doppeldecker mit 160 P. S. Mercedes-Motor, 2 sitzig.

Above: The L.F.G. Roland C.II was a fast and streamlined two-seater that served for only a relatively short time on the Western Front in 1916. This aircraft type could hold its own in a dogfight against the Allied fighter aircraft types it faced and its crews were very offensive minded in the air.

Below: A line up of Roland "Walfisch" of Kasta 8 sometime in Spring, 1916. The esprit de corps of the aviators is evident in their posing on top of their aircraft. On the very far left, marked with a large X, one of the aviators sitting on top of that plane could be Manfred von Richthofen.

Louis Breguet had designed successful aircraft before the war and the world's first separate military air service, the Aeronautique Militaire had purchased aircraft from him since its inception in 1910. At the start of the war, he brought along his personal aircraft and volunteered as a pilot.

On 2nd September Breguet spotted a large gap forming in the German forces as von Kluck swung further southeast along the Marne River, thus exposing his flank to the French Sixth Army that was moving in place alongside the BEF. This time, the Allies were able to better coordinate their efforts and utilizing the information from both British and French airmen the successful counter-attack known as the miracle of the Marne was possible.

These three early, critical battles ultimately

Above: The Roland C.II was very capable of success in a dogfight, and its aircrews took to decorating their aircraft in a personal and aggressive manner. Steve Anderson

were in large measure won or lost because of the significant (and accurate) reports supplied by the airmen to their commanding officers. The distrust and dismissal felt by the command staffs quickly went away as a result of the obvious successes in these significant battles.

Now commanders would not even consider to begin an attack without first extensive aerial reconnaissance and aerial photography of enemy positions. The French, immediately planned to increase the size of its air service from 20 squadrons to 50 by October 1914. By the summer of 1916 the RFC would be emphasizing the corps squadron concept and would put over 60% of its efforts into artillery shoots. Authors of the official history of the Royal Air Force in the First World War, Raleigh and Jones would write:

"Its first duty was reconnaissance. All its other and later uses were consequences of this central purpose, and were forced on it by the hard logic of events."

By late 1915 wireless transmitters were a common feature in observation aircraft, which dramatically improved their capabilities. However, the missions still required an aircraft to circle above the target which would be tedious, exhausting work with constant risk of being shot down by ground fire or being attacked by an enemy fighter. Another danger was actually being hit by the artillery shells being lobbed at the target since often the aircraft flew at a lower altitude than the maximal altitude reached by some of the artillery shells being fired. Lt. Alan Dore of 43 Sqdn. RFC wrote:

"LIne patrol. Clouds very low and snowstorms. [forcing him to fly at low altitude]Tremendous bombardment of Vimy Ridge in progress. Once I felt the concussion of a big howitzer shell pass so near that the whole aeroplane shuddered as though

Above: American Air Service reconnaissance units used the Salmson 2A2, a French designed and built aircraft with very good performance. The aircraft gave its crews great confidence in combat; note the two German crosses as victory markings by the gunners position. Also note the several fabric patches placed to repair bullet holes from combat have also been decorated with German crosses.

Left: Two aircrews stand beside a USAS Breguet bomber, these units were a very key force within William Mitchell's air armada at the end of the war.

Above: The Salmson 2A2 reconnaissance aircraft was sturdy, fast, and maneuverable. It was unusual for a WWI aircraft in that it had a radial engine; unlike later radial engines it was water-cooled. Steve Anderson

struck. Later I actually saw a shell come up and pass by me on its way to the Germans. It seems like a swiftly moving ball of black."

2nd Lt. C. Darly-Pine of 16 Sqdn. RFC remembered:

"One of the problems was anti-aircraft fire and shells coming from our own barrages, especially during an attack when we had to carry out contact patrols. I remember once feeling the heat from a 17-inch shell-like a blast from hell-which knocked my aircraft sideways and another time when my machine was actually hit. This shell passed through the fuselage, just behind my legs. I knew nothing about it-no doubt it was one of the many buffets I received on the trip. When I got out after landing, my mechanic said,'You've been lucky, Sir!' and pointed out a hole in the canvas of the nacelle with charred edges on both sides where a red-hot 3-inch shell had passed through…"

There were a myriad of manners which could bring the two-seater crew down: anti-aircraft fire, engine malfunction, attack by enemy fighters, being hit by one of the thousands of artillery shells lobbed into the air on any given mission, but no matter how it happened:

"It was always the same', wrote a soldier who saw many such episodes, 'We knew they were both still alive up there, but that they were going to die in flames in fifteen seconds, in ten seconds, in five second…We could never take our eyes from that long streak of smoke in the sky." John W.S. Gilchrist

Photo reconnaissance missions were made such that the entire length of the Western Front would be seen in mosaics of photos, again and again searching for changes in troop concentrations or valuable targets such as ammunition dumps or supply depots. The improvement in cameras during the war meant that at a height of 15,000 feet the photos had such

Above: An RE 8 in flight from the perspective of an observer in a second RE8.

Left: The RE8 was a workhorse for the corps squadrons of the RFC and RAF, it was used in a variety roles: bombing, reconnaissance, artillery spotting, close ground support and others.

Above: This German aircrew appear quite confident in their Halberstadt CL.II ground attack aircraft.

clarity and detail that individual footprints could sometimes be discerned.

Cecil Lewis wrote about his first reconnaissance mission in his classic *Sagittarius Rising*:

"So I set out that sunny afternoon, with a sergeant gunner in the front seat and I climbed towards the lines...There are times in life when the faculties seem to be keyed up to superhuman tension. You are not necessarily doing anything: but you are in a state of awareness, of tremendous alertness..Outwardly that day I was calm, busy keeping the trenches in the camera sight...but inside my heart was pounding and my nerves straining, waiting for something...Would Archie get the range? Would the dreaded Fokker appear? Would the engine give out? It was the fear of the unseen, the inescapable, the imminent hand of death which might, from moment to moment be ruthlessly laid upon me...Nobody could stand the strain indefinitely, ultimately it reduced you to a dithering state, near to imbecility."

Yet, day after day numerous patrols ranged over the trenches on missions that were deemed critical by the corps commanders. Aviators went on, until they were lost or could not stand the mental strains so eloquently expressed by Lewis.

Probably the most dangerous assignment given to the two-seater crews of the First World War was that of infantry contact patrol. Once an attack had begun, the featureless Western Front offered few landmarks with which to identify how far the troops had advanced or which parts of the battlefield were being contested.

Especially important was to direct the artillery fire at the remaining enemy positions but not at your own troops. These patrols required that the aircrew fly at extremely low altitudes, putting them at great risk from small arms fire from the ground.

In addition, often their own infantry units were very reluctant to reveal their positions using the prearranged signals(often a certain colored flare, or strips of cloth laid out in a letter or pattern). This

Above: The RE 8 was nicknamed the "Harry Tate", after a popular Scottish comedian. The types performance did not easily lend it to being a "fighter" aircraft. However, on 9th June 1918 the experienced crew of Roderick Armstrong and Frank Mart of 3 Sqdn. RNAS took on the inexperienced crew of Kuesler/Mullenbach of Shlasta 13 and forced them to land behind British lines. Steve Anderson

meant that the aircrew would have to fly repeated patterns over the same area, making them a choice target for ground fire or a swift attack from above by an enemy fighter.

Similar to the contact patrols, ground attack or strafing attacks against enemy positions was terrifying for the pilots because they could no longer range at higher altitudes, safe from ground fire. Instead they had the feeling that they had been ordered to fly directly into the inferno. Arthur Gould Lee was a pilot in the RAF who wrote in a letter to his wife:

"To make sure of your target you have to expose yourself to the concentrated fire of dozens of machine guns and hundreds of rifles. Compared with this, Archie is practically a joke...I've got to admit it gives me the shakes, With so many guns firing you

feel every time you dive that it's bound to be your last...That spell of low strafing has knocked some of the stuffing out of me. I don't get the same thrill out of flying as I used to do. Things have changed so much. So many chaps have gone, and half the people in the mess are strangers. I've been longer in the squadron than anybody and now I realize I've had enough. I feel a sort of waning of the spirit, and I shan't grumble if I'm now for home."

The overall contributions of these unsung heroes, these forgotten warriors of the air services of all the nations involved in the First World War should not be underestimated. It was these courageous aviators who ultimately made the biggest contributions to their respective nation's efforts and far too often paid the ultimate price.

An Experiment Into the Future

Above: HMS *Furious* in its initial state, with a take-off deck in front. Note the large crane available to retrieve floatplanes that took off utilizing a special dolly mechanism, the wheeled aircraft would have to fly to a land-based airfield or ditch in the sea nearby a small vessel.

H.M.S. *Furious* was a modified *Courageous* class battlecruiser launched in August 1916 and commissioned in June 1917. The ship was modified into an aircraft carrier while still under construction.

Her forward turret was removed and in its place a large hangar was placed in the forecastle (capable of holding ten aircraft). Above the hangar a 160 ft. "flying-off" deck was constructed. Aircraft had to be hoisted by crane from the hangar and placed onto the flight deck.

Even floatplanes could be flown off the deck using a four-wheel trolley that ran down a midline track built within the flight deck.

For non-float airplanes to return to H.M.S. *Furious*, they would have to fly around the funnel and superstructure and then hover above the flight deck in order to proceed to land. This was obviously less than ideal, but more on that later.

Because of the inordinate challenges brought about for landing, H.M.S. *Furious* returned to her builders, Armstrong Whitworth's Low Walker shipyard, in Newcastle upon Tyne for further alterations in November 1917.

The rear turret was then removed, and another hangar built with a 300 ft. long landing deck built upon it. However, less than a handful of landings were attempted which proved there was severe turbulence from the funnel and supra-structure, so no further attempts were made.

However, H.M.S. *Furious* was the world's first

Above: A good overhead view of HMS *Furious* demonstrates the addition of the landing platform in the rear of the ship, also noted is the heated, smoke filled, and turbulent air that would be found by the pilots trying to land there.

A close up view shows the distinct front (taking off) and rear (landing) decks. The two curved platforms on either side of the ship were used to move the aircraft from the rear to the forward area for taking off.

Above: A nice "portrait" of HMS *Furious* at anchor, displaying its zig-zag camouflage to good advantage.

operational aircraft carrier in the modern sense and as such was the experiment that launched the naval air services that would follow in the future. As the naval air services improved their capabilities, naval warfare would change and in the future it would be the aircraft carrier, not the battleship, that would become the most dominant naval warship in the fleet.

From the onset of the war, the RNAS worked towards eliminating the threats to the fleet and England itself from attack by the world's first terror weapon- Germany's zeppelins. The other chief assignments the RNAS would fulfill during the war was anti-submarine patrols and reconnaissance for the fleet. Seaplanes were used from a variety of bases on the English coast as well as from bases that would find the RNAS flying over the Adriatic, the Mediterranean Sea and coastal waters around Africa as well.

However, as the war progressed, the ascendency of an aircraft carrier as the superior means of projecting naval air power became clear to the admiralty. Therefore, the H.M.S. Furious would develop into the means to test and develop the potential for this new arm of the navy.

A brief timeline for the trials aboard H.M.S. *Furious*:

June 1917: operational service began with three Short 184 seaplanes with folding wings and five Sopwith Pups, which were difficult to move around the ship. Pilot's flying past initially saw no way to land safely back onto the ship, the takeoffs were not difficult as the *Furious* had a top speed of 31 knots, and aircraft could swiftly ascend as the *Furious* steamed into the wind.

2 August 1917: A South African Sqdn. Commander Edwin Dunning, DSC flying Sopwith Pup N6452 became the first pilot to land aboard a moving ship at sea. The *Furious* maintained 25 knots, headed into the wind while Dunning had to fly around the ship's superstructure and then tried to match the ship's speed while fellow RNAS pilots grabbed onto rope toggles hanging from below the aircraft to help steady the aircraft,. Dunning then cut his engine and landed!

7 August 1917: Dunning landed once again, but damaged his aircraft in the process. Later that day he took off in another Pup to try again, this time as he came around the supra-structure and swung over to hover over the front deck, he was too high. He waved off the landing party, opened his throttle to gain speed in order to climb for another go around, however he stalled, his aircraft bounced off the ship and fell off the starboard side. The aircraft was recovered, but tragically, Dunning had drowned before he could be rescued.

After review of these trials, a new landing deck in the rear of the ship was to be installed. Captain of the *Furious*, Wilmat Nicholson, thought this idea was less than optimal:" Eddy currents aft render landings more dangerous than forward." His advice went unheeded.

Above: It is the 2nd of August 1917 and Sqdn Commander Edwin Dunning is about to land on the forward deck of HMS *Furious*. To accomplish this feat he had to fly around the ship's superstructure and bring his aircraft to a hover and then stop his engine. Note the men rushing to help stabilize his aircraft by grabbing hold of several large rope toggles below his lower wings.

Below: Dunning is surrounded by joyful comrades after his successful landing.

Above: It is 7th August 1917 and Dunning is trying to repeat his success. Tragically he was not successful. Note the number of people trying to help stop his Sopwith Pup.

Below: Dunning careens over the side of HMS *Furious*. It seems likely that he was knocked unconscious as his aircraft hit the water and he drowned before help could reach him.

Above: Because of the tragic death of Dunning and the obvious dangers of trying to land on the front deck, a rear landing deck was added and a new system was devised to control the landing aircraft.

Above: These experiments would prove unsuccessful as most aircraft were damaged on landing because of profound turbulence caused by the superstructure of the ship.

Above: Sqdn. Commander Edwin Dunning circles HMS *Furious* before making the first successful landing on an aircraft carrier, note that he will have to come around the ship's superstructure and land on the forward "taking off" deck. James Field

Sopwith Pups and Sopwith 1½ Strutters were transferred on board to begin landing trials. Rear Admiral P.F. Phillimore, Admiral Commanding Aviation, was on board as a witness. As predicted, the trials were a complete failure. One of the pilots, Lt. W.G. Moore, summed up the trials "They just dropped on the deck like shot partridges."(Treadwell, *The First Naval Air War*, p.68)

However, *Furious* was not to be denied its further place in history. Force F.7 sailed on 17 July 1918, with H.M.S. *Furious* escorted by destroyers and several cruisers to begin the first attack by aircraft flying from a carrier flight deck in history. Two flights of Sopwith Camels, (seven aircraft in

total) were launched to attack the Zeppelin sheds at Tondern, Denmark. The attack was a success, destroying the Zeppelins L54 and L60 inside the sheds at their airbase. None of the aircraft were recovered, only two of the camels were able to return to the *Furious*, but they ditched alongside the ship since landing back onto the ship was nearly impossible.

As a tribute to the brave man who first landed back on board ship at sea, the Dunning Memorial Cup is awarded annually to the officer who is considered to have contributed the most to further aviation within the Fleet during that year.

Above: A good image of two Sopwith Pups on the front deck of HMS *Furious*. Because the ship could reach 30 knots, take off from the ship under speed and with a direction into the wind was not difficult.

Below: Seven of these Camels crowd the deck of the HMS *Furious* as it heads towards naval history with the successful launch against the German Zeppelin base at Tondern, Germany.

Some modifications to the front deck can be noted in this image of the new RNAS fighter, the modified Sopwith Camel 2F1 seen here.

Above: The first flight of Sopwith Camels successfully destroyed two German Zeppelins, L 54 and L 60, that had been located in the largest shed at Tondern. Steve Anderson.

Facing Page, Above: Three of the seven Tondern raiders fly away from the HMS *Furious*. Note the different details of the ship compared to the prior artwork. James Field

Facing Page, Below: A Sopwith Camel roars off the launching deck of HMS *Furious*.

Death's Hussar

Above: Early in the war Nungesser helped capture a German Mors staff car and for the duration of the war used it as a personal vehicle.

Aviation historian Herbert Molloy Mason, Jr. titled his chapter concerning Charles Nungesser "The Iron Viking". In that chapter he described Nungesser in this manner:

"In 1909, when he was sixteen years old, Nungesser already had the build of a cultivated athlete: he stood five-feet-nine and weighed 150 pounds-weight distributed and hardened by a childhood devoted to cycling, boxing, swimming, weight lifting and long distance running. His large Norman head was topped with thick blond hair... his eyes, deep set and bright blue, looked out over a strong straight-ridged nose. He lips were firm, the jaw square and outthrust, dimpled in the middle. The face as a whole had a strong Scandinavian cast, heritage from Northern ancestors nine centuries past."

Nungesser would need every ounce of both his physical and mental strength as both would be tested to and often, literally past the breaking point during his service to France in the First World War.

By 1908, the headstrong and adventurous young man convinced his mother to allow him to travel to Rio de Janeiro in order to find an uncle. It would take Nungesser about four years to actually find his uncle.By that time he had made his way to Buenos Aires where he learned to be an auto mechanic and then proved to be a very capable, cup-winning race car driver.

At some point, he was mesmerized by watching a barnstorming French aviator go through an acrobatic routine. Naturally, Nungesser simply then had to take flying lessons and learn to challenge himself through flight.

Even in South America, the papers were filled with stories of Europe and the ever-louder drumbeats of impending war. Nungesser made his way back to France and offered his services as an aviator. At the start of the war, there were more trained aviators than aircraft and so his offer was declined. Nungesser joined the Second Regiment of Hussars and on 3rd September 1914 found himself with a fellow cavalryman and two infantrymen lost and isolated from their units during the chaotic retreat to the Marne.

There were German patrols everywhere and Nungesser was trying to find an escape route back to his unit. A large, elegant Mors touring sedan with fluttering staff corps pennants approached Nungesser and his comrades on the road.The Frenchmen quickly leaped to the side of the road and let loose a fusillade of carbine fire. The car veered off the road and into the ditch. Four ranking German officers lay dead in the car. After searching and taking all papers, maps, and anything that looked of value from the dead Germans; the Frenchmen hopped into the car with Nungesser behind the wheel. He drove at breakneck speed towards where he thought the French lines were.

As they raced along, the group was shot at by

Above: Nungesser displays a portion of his first confirmed victory, scored in the Voison.

German units who saw French soldiers in the car, and the group was shot at by French units who saw a speeding German staff car. As they crossed into the French lines the group was arrested as spies. Nungesser protested and said they had important information for French staff officers to review. He was brought before the commanding general of the 53rd division.

A quick review of the materials provided by Nungesser gave the French details about the

Below: Nungesser beside his new Nieuport 11 during the battle of Verdun.

Above: A low flying Nieuport demonstrates at exceptionally low altitude. Nungesser's flight at a German aerodrome would likely have given a similar view to the Germans on the ground.

Above: By the end of the war, Nungesser would be the most decorated French pilot of the war.

upcoming German advance plans. The general not only congratulated Nungesser, he asked him to have lunch and awarded him the captured staff car as a prize. The general also joked about how Nungesser was now a 'Mors Hussar(a play on the French word- mort, death).

The general awarded Nungesser the Medaille Militaire, the highest award he could receive at the time. Most importantly, the general promised to help Nungesser with his most urgent desire- a transfer to the aviation service.

After official military flight training, his first assignment was to escadrille V.B. 106(Voison bombing) and Nungesser promptly displayed his lack of fear in the air. His aircraft would often come back with extensive damage from anti-aircraft ground fire during his 53 bombing missions, comprised of both day and early evening sorties and completed in a very short timespan.

On 31 July 1915 Nungesser was supposed to be on a stand-by basis and assigned to some ground duties (which he detested). Nungesser noted that the unit had just received a new Voison aircraft, one that was not configured to carry numerous bombs but instead had a Hotchkiss machine gun mounted for the observer to fire: likely a machine that was to act as an escort on future bombing missions.

Without authorization of any kind, Nungesser took the aircraft up for a flight eager to put its fighter-like qualities to the test. He caught up with a

Above: An extraordinary photo showing the French naval office, Le Pieur, inventor of the air-to-air rocket system used during the attack on German observation balloons, discussing the system with the French pilots who would fly the aircraft.

flight of five German two-seat Albatros aircraft that were bombing targets in nearby Nancy. Nungesser dove into the formation, scattered the aircraft and along with his gunner downed one of the Albatros aircraft for his first confirmed victory.

His angry commander, because of Nungesser's disregard for his official assignment, disciplined Nungesser to eight days house arrest for his insubordination in taking the Voison, but also awarded him the Croix de Guerre for the downed German aircraft. His house arrest was eased by gifts of food and wine from grateful citizens of Nancy

who had been spared from the German bombing raid.

Even more importantly, after the eight days were over, Nungesser was transferred back to aviation school in order to become a pursuit pilot. Upon completion of his training he was given a brand new Nieuport 11 fighter and told to report to escadrille N. 65, which was one of the newest fighter squadrons.

Nungesser simply could not contain his joy, as he flew over his new airfield. He elected to put on a dazzling and impressive display of aerobatics. His new commander Capt. Louis Gonnet-Thomas was

Below: Nungesser pictured on the day of the mission.

Above: Nungesser's commander chastised him for performing aerobatics over the airfield, telling Nungesser to impress the Germans instead, Nungesser promptly flew over the lines to a German airfield and did just that! Note the German Fokker fighters in the background. John Richards

Above: For a time, Nungesser flew with the Americans in escadrille N.124, he is seen here with William Thaw.

Above: Nungesser poses with his Nieuport for a photo while with N.124.

unimpressed.

His commander suggested that Nungesser should try to impress and frighten the enemy with such antics. Nungesser ordered that his Nieuport's gas tank be refilled and then immediately took off. Nungesser crossed the lines and found a German aerodrome whereupon he repeated his aerobatic routine, this time over the German airfield!

Above: Nungesser would often receive the newest type of Nieuport fighter, which he and his mechanic Pouchon would modify to their liking.

Above: Nungesser flew to several Allied airfields on the Flanders front to show off his aircraft and its markings so as not to have another air combat with a British aircraft.

Below: Nungesser in his Nieuport fighter on a British airfield (note the British aircraft in the background): the extra red-white-blue stripes on the wings.

Above: Nungesser scores one of his victories in dramatic fashion. Steve Anderson

Nungesser then returned to his airfield and confidently strode up to Capt. Gonnet-Thomas and emphatically stated that his orders had been carried out exactly as he had said. Yet again, Nungesser was placed on eight days house arrest, this time for unwarranted risk to his aircraft and himself.

Two days later, on the 28th November 1915, Nungesser wrangled permission to take a test flight of his aircraft to make certain it was in good condition. No sooner than he had climbed above his airfield, Nungesser spotted two German observation aircraft. Nungesser continued to climb above them and then maneuvered into a favorable position and dove to attack. One of the Albatros aircraft dove away while the other turned into Nungesser and the observer held a steady fire from his parabellum machine gun. They turned and fired, turned and fired until Nungesser closed within 30 feet and with another burst of his Lewis gun, caused the German pilot into a sudden and violent dive.

Nungesser later wrote what happened next:

"The observer, still alive, clung desperately to the mounting ring to which his machine gun was attached. Suddenly the mounting ripped loose from the fuselage and was flung into space, taking with it the helpless crewman. He clawed frantically at the air, his body working convulsively like a man on a trapeze. I had a quick glimpse of his face before he tumbled away through the clouds...it was a mask of horror."

This time, Nungesser's commander commuted the remainder of his detention and recommended him for yet another commendation.

Nungesser was now clearly being recognized as one of the best pilots in the French AIr Service. Along with other notables such as Navarre, Vedrines, Garros, and Guynemer. Therefore, it was not unusual that Nungesser was summoned from the front lines to test fly a new aircraft design: the Ponnier M.1 biplane.

Above: After being forced to shoot down a British fighter that continued to attack him despite Nungesser's French cockades, he would always put numerous red/white/blue stripes on his aircraft to try to prevent such a tragedy from happening again. Seweryn Fleischer

The airplane was unstable and inherently lethal to fly. However, that was not yet known when Nungesser took off on 29th January 1916 for a test flight. Spectators spoke of his crash as "frightful" and Nungesser was not expected to survive at first. He had broken both legs, smashed and unhinged his jaw, destroyed the roof of his mouth and had multiple internal injuries. This would be the first serious crash with horrific resultant injuries that Nungesser would suffer in the war, but it was far from his last.

"The Iron Viking" left the hospital in only two weeks and in eight, short weeks he had reported back to N.65 for duty. He was hobbled and walking was only capable with a cane. Sometimes, he had his ground crew carry him to and from his aircraft. Once inside the cockpit, Nungesser flew as brilliantly, and as recklessly as always.

Nungesser and N.65 now found themselves a part of the horrific battle of Verdun. Nungesser's spirit was undaunted. As a testament to his inner

strength and relentless stamina, he volunteered for a special mission on 22 May 1916. He would be one of eight pilots to arm their Nieuport fighters with the new LePrieur rockets.

The mission was to simultaneously attack eight German observation balloons to deprive the enemy of directing artillery fire against a French counter attack. The aviators proved quite successful as six of the eight, including Nungesser, destroyed their targets utilizing the air-to-air rocket system.

During a particularly frenzied air combat that summer, Nungesser faced two very "expertly" flown German Fokker fighters. After he was shot in the mouth by one of the German bullets, Nungesser stuffed his silk scarf into his mouth and bit down to tamponade the bleeding and carried on in the fight! Some historians believe that one of the Fokkers was flown by Oswald Boelcke himself.

Shortly after that air battle, Nungesser had another extended fight and downed two German Aviatik two-seaters behind French lines. Nungesser's

Above: A post-war portrait of Nungesser, again note the number of medals he received from a grateful nation.

Above: Nungesser with his fiancee Conseuelo Hatmaker, they married in 1923 and separated in 1926.

aircraft had also sustained damage during the dogfight which resulted in Nungesser crash-landing near his victims. As a result of the crash Nungesser sustained a broken nose and a broken jaw. He dislocated one of his knees and re-broke one of his legs.

As a result, he was forced into sick leave and in response Nungesser assigned himself to escadrille N.124 and began to fly sorties with the Americans as soon as he could. Again, he found himself often having to be carried from his aircraft after a mission, too exhausted to hobble with his cane at that point. He certainly made an impression with his American allies as Lafayette escadrille historian Dennis Gordon quoted one of them:

"Last night we had Numgesser here for dinner...a wonderful chap, blond and handsome, blue eyes, and rather square, clean-cut face; slightly sandy mustache; a striking feature is his smile which reveals two solid rows of gold teeth. He has lost all of his own teeth and wears a silver jaw; also walks with a limp- his left leg a little out of kilter."

While there, on 21st July Nungesser scored

his tenth victory. In the fall, he returned to N.65 which was now stationed along the front lines in the Somme region. Nungesser managed to shoot down two airplanes and one balloon in a single day. However, shortly after that success Nungesser crashed after taking off on a mission. He again broke his jaw, and this time the surgeons also operated again on his left leg, since it had not mended well the first time. This involved them breaking the leg and repairing it anew.

Then the latest repair of his jaw became infected, which necessitated opening the incision, irrigation, drainage and constant cauterization of dead tissue to prevent worsening infection. The doctors would all comment on how Nungesser had a super-human capacity to suffer through pain.

Even Nungesser realized he needed to take an extended time in order to heal. And yet, with his score at 21 as the year ended, Nungesser also did not like the idea of fellow aces such as Guynemer and Fonck adding to their scores while he remained "idle".

Therefore, he once again worked out a temporary

assignment to another escadrille, this time it was V.116: which was a two-seater observation/photographic unit. Nungesser brought along his Nieuport fighters and flew from their field during the morning. Then in the afternoon he reported to the nearby hospital in Dunkerque for treatment. This arrangement lasted from May to August of 1917. During that time, Nungesser would score regularly with six confirmed victories in May alone.

After downing a German Gotha bomber on 26 June 1917 Nungesser was attacked by a British fighter plane. At first, Nungesser merely flew in defensive circles so as to show the British pilot the red-white-blue roundels indicating an Allied aircraft. Still the opposing pilot pressed his attack, Nungesser assumed that it was a German pilot flying a captured aircraft and shot the fighter down.

Upon landing, Nungesser was visibly shaken and upset to learn that it had indeed been a British pilot. Nungesser instructed that his aircraft would now have broad red/white/blue stripes painted on the wings to help prevent another such incident. The unfortunate friend-on-friend battle was also ironic in that Nungesser had earlier received the British Military Cross for having saved a British observation aircraft that was under a fierce attack by several German fighters.

These stripes of the Allied colors were not the only special markings on Nungesser's aircraft. During the First World War French escadrilles would decorate the sides of their fuselages with a symbol that was unique for their squadron, all pilots sharing that same escadrille symbol.

However, Nungesser had his own, unique, macabre decoration of a black heart, with a skull and coffin and candles that he painted on all his aircraft. This distinct heraldry was to signify that Nungesser totally embraced his identification as Death's Hussar.

Even with his demonstrable success during his assignment to the Dunkerque sector, he finally had to recognize that even for the great Nungesser, he had had enough. The end of summer and early autumn of 1917, Nungesser was to spend most of his time in Paris as he sought to "rebuild" himself physically and no doubt mentally as well.

Even with the deprivations forced upon the city because of the war, Paris was a special place for Allied soldiers on leave. However, the combination of Paris and the attitude of an aviator was a special combination. The noted writer Jacques Mortane pondered what made the aviator such a unique breed in the armed forces of the First World War:

"The aviator is a special kind of soldier. He is allowed greater license than the poilu and serves under a less strict discipline. He is regarded as more of an artist than a worker. His officers give him orders and he obeys, but they know that a pilot needs inspiration to do great things. His life may well be more agreeable than that of the front-line soldier, but it is also more eventful...the courage of the infantryman is that of the group. The pilot is a solitary hero. He has no one beside him. He cannot share the contagion of battle fever. He could turn around, fly home and dream up all sorts of excuses. In the sky, he can do what he likes; no one is making him fight. Simple devotion to duty is all that compels him to seek out danger and so often emerge triumphant." quoted in Sumner, *Kings Of The Air*, p.107

A French pilot, Jean Beraud-Villars had this to say:

"The fighting spirit of our service stems from our independence and imagination...from our young COs and our pilots, younger still, who love to fight and enjoy life in equal measure. We provide a refuge for anyone unhappy with the strict discipline of other units, who loathes all the boredom and hanging around, but loves danger and adventure and wishes to serve. These individualists come to us."

In his book, Ian Sumner wrote:

"Manufacturers like Voisin, Nieuport and Spad courted the pilots who flew their planes. 'Leave was introduced in 1915,' recalled aircraft manufacturer Gabriel Voisin,'and the first chaps were expected to arrive in Paris thirsting for liberty...In 1914 I had bought a little house on the Boulevard Lannes...I held the house-warming in 1915 and all my guests were aces...The large number of young ladies in attendance soon made Voisin's house the social center for off-duty pilots, as well as attracting police attention. But when the flics came calling, it was Charles Nungesser...who took control: ' With his blonde hair, battered face, china-blue eyes, mocking smile and scarred chin, he had the bearing, the self-confidence and the voice.' He calmly drew the gendarmes aside and within minutes had them drinking a toast to fighter pilots. Furthermore, confessed the owner,' when dawn crept upon us, the ladies were wearing the policeman's uniforms... Nungesser later attempted to defend the roistering: 'They're not women. They're pals. You have a good time together. All aviators are playboys. We fly fighter planes. We hunt down a Boche or fly a mission...You come home and head to Paris for a couple of days. That is all there is to it." Sumner, p.144

Nungesser had a special arrangement with the Nieuport company manufacturing his fighter aircraft. He would be issued the first aircraft of a

Above: A modern replica Nieuport sporting Nungesser's personal insignia.

new type and Nungesser, along with his faithful mechanic Pauchon would often modify the aircraft and sometimes would have a variant that Nieuport would then go on to produce. Nungesser continued to fly Nieuport fighters much longer than any of the other Fench aces who switched to the Spad VII and Spad XIII as soon as they were available.

On 16th August 1917 Nungesser scored his thirtieth victory when he downed a Gotha bomber, his first victory in his new Spad fighter. Less than a month later, Guynemer would be lost and Nungesser would be the top ace of the French Air Force.

Shortly after Guynemer went missing, Nungesser too was lost to his comrades in the front line squadrons. Lousy weather was bad for fighter sorties, but it was perfect for providing an evening sortie in Paris. Because of his numerous injuries Nungesser now had to have his trusted mechanic Pouchon drive him, and the pair were often seen in Nungesser's prized Mors staff car. This evening, as the pair sped down the road towards the City of Lights, Pouchon had a heart attack and lost control of the speeding vehicle. It bounded off the road and smashed head on, at full speed into a tree. Pouchon was instantly killed, Nungesser once again broke his

fragile jaw and suffered numerous other injuries.

He would not return to escadrille Spa.65 until March 1918. Undaunted, his spirit literally unbroken, he would continue to be the same aggressive fighter pilot until the very end of the war. On 14th August Nungesser shot down four balloons, two before breakfast and then two more immediately after lunch!

Incredibly, the man who had so many injuries and almost countless crashes survived the war.

He would start a flying school, he would barnstorm across the United States and he would be in the news everywhere he went. Perhaps seeking even more fame, perhaps seeking just the challenge as to whether he could do what no other aviator had done: Nungesser took off, with his navigator Coli, from Le Bourget airfield early in the morning of 8th May 1927. His special aircraft, again adorned with his personal insignia, was last seen flying above the coast at Le Havre headed West.

They never reached their destination, Death's Hussar had finally, at long last begun a mission that he would not complete, Charles Nungesser and Raymond Coli were lost somewhere into the Atlantic Ocean.

Eagle of the Aegean

Above: "Rudi" von Eschwege, the Eagle of the Aegean.

It is fair to say that most avid first world war one aviation historians, as they research and delve into the events of military aviation during that war, end up having several "favorite" aviators that are likely not very well-known. This does not mean that the Red Baron, or George Guynemer or Albert Ball do not deserve their fame. It is just that, there are other pilots who were just as courageous and possibly even more deserving of some recognition for the feats that they accomplished, despite the daunting odds they faced and/or second rate equipment they were issued in which to face the enemy in combat.

One such person has to be, Ltn. Rudolf von Eschwege.

By the time Lt.von Eschwege (known to one and all of his comrades as Rudi) was transferred with FL.Abt.30 to support Germany's Bulgarian allies, he was a veteran and skilled pilot. He began his military flying career in two-seaters in July 1915, but by May 1916 he had been chosen to fly his unit's Fokker E-type fighter as an escort on reconnaissance missions. Rudi was then transferred to the Macedonia front in the fall of 1916 and would be the only German fighter pilot on that front(for some time).He would face aircraft from both the RNAS and the RFC, as well as French and Serbian aircraft.

He would face daunting odds of 10:1 in numbers of aircraft and be given a list of nearly impossible missions to complete as the sole fighter:

1)   Protect all German aircraft
2)   Intercept any Allied aircraft
3)   Protect the Bulgarian 10th division from aerial attacks along its 62 mile coastline and along the nearly 37 miles bordering the Struma River

He initially had a Fokker E-type monoplane to fly and scored his first victory over a Nieuport N12 from 2nd wing RNAS on 19 November 1916. He had to make 23 attacks against the solitary aircraft before achieving success because of almost innumerable gun stoppages. After this flight, von Eschwege always loaded his aircraft's guns by himself. After this success he would receive a Halberstadt fighter and before too long an Albatros DIII.

These improved aircraft, coupled with von Eschwege's skill and daring soon began his incredible career. The loud booming of heavy guns near Drama, Greece woke the personnel at FL.Abt.30's airfield on the morning of 20 May 1917. Rudi quickly took to the skies and noted that a RNAS Maurice-Farman observation plane was directing an intense barrage from nearby Royal Naval warships. However, the aircraft was escorted by seven fighters- a clear indication of the importance of the mission.

He flew off to the East, gained enough altitude above the British flight and then brought his aircraft around so that his attack would place the sun behind him. Only then did von Eschwege dive down against the daunting odds. His attack surprised the British

Above: Von Eschwege in an automobile with a canine friend.

Above: By the time of the British ruse, von Eschwege was flying this Albatros D.III.

Above: Although inaccurate in the depiction of von Eschwege flying a Halberstadt D.II, which he had flown earlier during his career, this image depicts the dramatic moment of the denotation of the bomb placed by the British in the dummy filled balloon basket. Wilf Hardy

escorts, Rudi calmly dispatched the Maurice-Farman observation plane on his first attack. He then continued his dive so as to escape the now hapless escorts and soon landed back at his airfield having completely disrupted the mission.

In a dogfight against two British B.E. aircraft, again in May 1917, Rudi was hit in his right arm by a burst from one of the observer's Lewis guns. Another bullet from that same burst had hit his fuel tank. Von Eschwege turned away from the dogfight, changed to his auxiliary fuel tank and then turned back to chase the British who had turned for home, no doubt with thoughts of how to tell the story of how they had brought down the Eagle of the Aegean! Von Eschwege calmly, despite his wound, caught up with the two British aircraft and shot one of the two down before he broke away to his home base and medical attention.

This portion of the Macedonia front was known for its especially brutal landscapes and weather. Each of the two German aviation units had 90 horses and 30 wagons with which to bring needed supplies to the isolated airfields located on the rarely found suitable areas for flying.

The summer heat was so intense that missions were only flown in the early morning or late in the day, so that the aircraft could function.

The warfare in the area was also known for its unrestricted nature. The prior year, the Allies had flown bombing missions utilizing incendiary bombs in order to burn and destroy the important wheat crop of the area in an attempt to diminish the food supply to the Bulgarian troops.

In June 1917, a flight of two Henri Farman aircraft escorted by a Sopwith Baby seaplane was in the process of repeating that mission. This time, unlike 1916, von Eschwege was there and he destroyed one of the Henri Farman bombers and so harassed the other aircraft that the mission was abandoned and no other similar attack was tried again.

Rudi himself, was known by his fellow airmen as well as his opponents as being remarkably chivalrous in his behavior and was honored in that regard. For example, when he was able to down a RFC pilot, Lt.J.C.F. Owen, in his B.E.12 fighter near von Eschwege's Drama airfield, he landed and then personally took charge of the British pilot's capture: bringing him to his airfield and entertaining him there for a day or so. Von Eschwege then flew over the Allied lines to drop a message and a photo of Owen so that his family could be notified he was alive and in good health.

A new army commander to the front lines supposedly worried about how readily available his reconnaissance reports would be when he learned that there was only one fighter aircraft to fly escort on these missions. One must presume he was re-assured when he was told: "Yes, it is true, there is only one scout plane- but it is flown by von Eschwege"!

Although the Allies could not bring him out of the skies, a bout of malaria took von Eschwege away for recovery during the remainder of the summer and early fall of 1917.

When he returned to the battle, it seems that perhaps Rudi had caught "balloon fever" during his medical leave of absence. On 28th October 1917 he made his first attack on a captive balloon at Orljak, on the west bank of the Struma River. He needed to make four passes before he was able to set the balloon on fire.

On 9th November he damaged a balloon and killed the observer in his attack, but failed to ignite the balloon before his machine guns completely jammed.

On 15th November Rudi flamed another balloon of the 17th Kite Balloon Section at Orljak. On the 19th November, his attack on a balloon was foiled when the ground crew managed to winch the balloon to the ground before he could complete his attack. However, von Eschwege managed to shoot down one of the Sopwith fighters from the balloon's protective flight instead.

In an observation post north of Seres, at dawn on the following day, a Bulgarian officer watched the now famous Albatros DIII fighter approach an enemy balloon that was once again raised in the sky above Orljak, across the Struma River. He knew it had to be the Eagle of the Aegean, since there was only a single type of that aircraft on the front lines.

He also later reported that he noticed two unusual things about the Allied balloon; it was at a discernibly higher than normal altitude and there was no anti-aircraft fire at all. It was if the British were challenging von Eschwege to attack.

Indeed they were. Rudi lined up and dove as usual to close in upon the balloon. To make certain his shots counted, or in case there was a jammed gun after only the first few rounds, he closed in upon his prey.

It is actually not known if he even managed to fire his guns before a tremendous explosion lit up the early morning sky and almost instantly the balloon and von Eschwege disappeared together in the flames.

The British had determined to be rid of their erstwhile foe by any means possible. They had patched up a very old balloon for its last flight and loaded a large amount of munitions into the observer's basket along with a straw-dummy covered in an old flying coat and helmet with goggles.

As Rudi closed in, the bomb was detonated by a wire from the ground and the Eagle of the Aegean was gone. Later, the British buried Rudi with full military honors, and returned his personal effects with photos of the honorary funeral via a message and wreath which read in part to "our chivalrous foe".

Although relieved to be free of their all too-successful adversary, the British certainly betrayed their hypocrisy when an official account recalled:

"He came to his end as a result of a legitimate ruse of war, but there was no rejoicing among the pilots of the squadrons which had suffered from his activities. They would have preferred that he had gone down in fair combat."

Dogfighting

Above: At the beginning of the war, there were some aircraft capable of being fighter aircraft, but there was not a weapon suitable for use. These RNAS Bristol Scouts have small boxes on their fuselage sides which would be filled with large, weighted darts to drop on the enemy.

"The concentrated violence of
aerial dogfights
has to be experienced
to be known" Cecil Lewis

Since this book's title is The Art of the Dogfight it seems appropriate to devote at least one chapter to the specific concept of the aerial dogfight. Such an event had not happened before the start of the First World War and one must remember that in the beginning, the military aviators of the various belligerent nations did not really know what to expect as they went off to a large scale war in their small, frail aircraft in August, 1914.

The very first recorded "dogfight" is alleged to have occurred in Mexican skies sometime in late 1913 or early 1914. Two American mercenary pilots, Dean Lamb and Phil Rader, flying for opposing sides in the Mexican Revolution supposedly exchanged pistol fire without any discernible deleterious effects to either pilot or his respective aircraft. It

is not clear that this event actually took place or if this story was just that, a good old Western cowboy fabrication.

At the start of the war, the available aircraft were designed for reconnaissance and little else. The fledgling military aviators quickly became interested in devising means of attacking the enemy and doing more than simply filing reports. Improvised bombs were created and hastily improved in the field in order to be more effective. Other devices were also tried, such as releasing a number of flechettes upon the enemy troops below. And rather quickly, airmen began to carry rifles and then lightweight machine guns into the air in order to attack enemy aircraft.

Still, the effectiveness any aviator or his airplane in successfully attacking an enemy aircraft was limited by multiple factors:

Facing Page: The flight leader signals for the diving attack; hopefully there is no enemy flight waiting above and he is not leading his flight into a trap. George Evans

196

Left: There was no gun camera footage in WWI as there was in WWII. However, French ace George Guynemer had attached a small Kodak camera to a strut in front of his cockpit and this photo is of an Albatros fighter he is attacking.

Left: The classic dogfight; a Sopwith Camel has made a pass at a German Albatros while a German Fokker Triplane moves to get in position to attack the Britisher. Brian Knight

Above: An often seen, but actual photo of a two-seater being shot down, the photograph taken from a comrade.

The aircraft of 1914: the generally limited power plant capabilities of their engines limited their performance in maneuvering as well as their capability in being effectively armed

For the aviators themselves: there simply was no instruction booklet on how to actually attack an enemy aircraft, nor were the pilots themselves completely certain of acrobatics and the possibilities of how to maneuver their aircraft outside of several basic concepts- for example Pegoud had only recently proved that inverted flight was possible.

Another key factor in limiting the new art of dogfighting in 1914 and into 1915 was the fact that each side had so few aircraft. Pilot/observer crews could often perform several missions a day, every day for a week or more and never actually see an enemy aircraft during their sorties.

However, as the importance of aerial reconnaissance became clearly apparent following some of the significant successes in the early part of

the war, as well as the development of the elaborate trench systems of the Western Front which would limit the usefulness of cavalry; Some of the more far-sighted commanding officers encouraged the ideas of how to arm aircraft that were beginning to be discussed by frontline aviators, with the hope of denying the enemy their chances of aerial reconnaissance.

As recounted elsewhere in more detail, several French airmen were instrumental at initiating air combat. The most well-known was Roland Garros who, with some help, designed a system of steel deflector wedges placed on the inside of his aircraft's propellor that would deflect any bullet that did not safely pass through the moving blades. Because his Hotchkiss machine gun was bolted onto the fuselage in front of him, Garros could now fly directly at his enemy and fire in the same direction that he was headed.

Garros was alone in his Morane Saulnier Parasol

Above: An absolute classic image of a Sopwith Pup chasing an enemy. But does the pilot see the German Albatros above him in the clouds? Nixon Galloway

when he came upon a German Albatros two-seater observation aircraft. The German observer fired several shots from his carbine at the Frenchman as Garros approached'

"I [Garros] opened fire from thirty yards and quickly ran through the first clip. After the first few rounds I could see the enemy plane was in disorder, I recharged my machine gun three times in succession, firing continuously, keeping always above the enemy. Then, from 3,000 feet above the earth, the enemy plane began its fall, riddled like a sieve. Quickly it took fire and wrapped in an immense sheet of flames it fell spinning to the ground Twenty-five seconds later it struck in a huge burst of smoke. The entire flight had lasted no more than ten minutes, although it seemed much longer... Afterwards, I drove to see the debris...It would be futile to try to express my satisfaction at such an overwhelming success, despite the anguish I felt at seeing those crisply burned bodies. It was tragic,

appalling" Roland Garros

From the very beginning, some very basic principles of dogfighting were established: attack from a position of advantage and use superior firepower to overwhelm your enemy. Also established was that a dogfight was generally very short in duration, even though it could seem quite a long time to the combatants themselves. Finally, to lose a dogfight in the First World War generally meant a tortured and grisly end for the vanquished aviators, since for most of the First World War none of the aviators had parachutes (observers in balloons did have parachutes as well as German pilots in the last few months of the war).

Before too long, the capture of Garros's aircraft allowed the Germans to make use of his device. Instead, Anthony Fokker installed a working synchronized gun onto his single-seat monoplane, transforming his M.5 to the newly christened E.I fighter.

Above: A book published in 1933, *Death in the Air*, had numerous photographs that were reputed to have been taken in action. Decades later the photos would eventually be revealed as faked photos using model aircraft and elaborate lighting. Still, the photos may well be the closest that exist to how a WWI dogfight actually looked.

Right: Another of the Cockburn-Lange photographs.

Above: A flight of JG III Fokker D VIIs dive into a formation of British SE5a fighters and the close maneuvering begins. Brian Knight
Facing Page: A contemporary painting of a very common WWI dogfight as a lone aircraft is pounced upon in a surprise attack by another aircraft that had been hiding in a could bank. Artist unknown

Max Immelmann , one of the first successful German pilots in the ensuing Fokker Scourge, would become famous for his "Immelmann turn", a maneuver he adapted/developed in order to "bounce" upon the enemy from above and quickly regain the advantage of altitude and combine that height with the chance to pounce again on the enemy target if needed, no matter which way the enemy had turned in an attempt to escape his first attack: the beginning of the dogfight.

Following the well-published early successes of German pilots utilizing the Fokker monoplane, another of the new fighter aces, Oswald Boelcke wrote:

"They[enemy pilots] treat my single-seater with a holy respect.They bolt as quickly as they can."

Thus, in order to succeed, the German fighter pilots would need to devise methods in which to surprise their enemy and not allow them the chance to escape.

Boelcke would become the first acknowledged master of tactics in the air. Stalking the enemy aircraft via cloud cover, gaining an altitude advantage, using the sun to shield you from detection by the enemy and most of the other frequently discussed tactics began with him.

He would be credited with establishing the Boelcke dicta, which outlined the best ways in which to engage the enemy in aerial combat. So now, there was a primer on how to fly in a dogfight. "Best practices" were being established and to ignore these principles would be to invite a catastrophic result. What is not often written is something else that Boelcke wrote:

"Foolish acts of bravery only bring death."

And here is the basic difference from the reality of air combat in the First World War. The writers of propaganda, the writers trying to raise morale in their home audiences, the writers of "good" stories quickly and quite purposely established the fiction of aerial jousting by these new, knights of the air. The stories of how the combatant foes

Above: By the middle of the war, the Germans had established specific Jastaschule (fighter schools), the world's first Top Gun units. The units used captured Allied aircraft to fight in mock combats to teach the fledgling German fighter pilots how to best their opponents at the front. This photo shows two captured Nieuport fighters used at the school.

Above: A Jasta 5 Albatros drops into the desired six-clock position of a Sopwith Camel from 10 Sqdn. RNAS. Mark Miller

Above: Most WWI Dogfights were actually more of a zoom attack from higher altitude, often surprising the target aircraft and then diving away to escape any retaliation. The French Spad was well-suited to this type of attack. Keith Burns

would circle endlessly around each other and then wave each to each other as they flew off back home was essentially nonsense. The dogfights of the First World War (also referred to as melees, and furballs amongst other epithets) were usually brief. They usually consisted of one pilot (or flight of aircraft later in the war) trying to pounce upon an enemy and then quickly speed away while the defender attempted a maneuver to shake off the initial attack.

One estimate states that 80% of casualties in the war had flown fewer than 20 frontline missions. In other words, the newly arrived replacement pilots were ripe for the harvesting because they could be surprised in the first attack and did not know that the best defensive maneuver was to turn into your attacker, or simply panicked at the start of the fight.

In fact, many of the veteran pilots when writing about their wartime experiences mention how it was usually easy to tell if the foe had experience or not during the initial moments of a dogfight. And the

Above: Another photo from a Jastaschule shows a captured Spad fighter in German markings.

clever pilots who were to survive would often break off an attack if the enemy appeared to be "talented" and instead would go looking for easier prey.

The leading Allied ace of the war, the Frenchman Rene Fonck would earn six confirmed victories in a single day. Not a single one was scored while engaging in the romantic-styled dogfight so often found in the fictional prose written about the air

Above: One of the fears that pilots faced during a melee or dogfight was that of a collision. Charles Faust

Above: Sometimes a dogfight that began at altitude would continue as the aircraft approached altitudes that were barely above the ground. Brian Knight

war. He used his Spad's superior speed and capability to dive at high speed because of its sturdy design, as well as his skilled marksmanship to great advantage.

His first three victories of the day are exemplary of the more typical air combats in the war. As quoted by the renowned French aviation historian David Mechin, an article in the popular French news journal, Le Petit Parisien, relayed the first successful sortie of the day as follows:

"Fonck, traveling in the lead, heads to the Moreuil-Montdidier sector...He signals then to his comrades and goes straight ahead by diving on the first, From the first burst, the Boche falls in flames, Fonck has already passed, presses on the left and returns by a curve to the second Boche which, turns to the right to return to its own lines. He thus appears to Fonck three quarters before and a little below, and takes five bullets: Fonck puts him down, Only ten seconds passed between the two victories. The third enemy remained behind...He [Fonck] follows him for a while and pretends to give way as if he were returning to our lines. The Boche lets himself be caught...Fonck, when he sees it is in range, makes a right turn, approaches his opponent face-on and shoots it down with a short burst. The three Germans fell almost in the same place, in one square kilometer in a minute and a half, and Fonck sent them all down with, in all, twenty-two bullets."

An experienced fighter pilot, one could even say professional, such as Fonck could wreak havoc upon an enemy flight in a short period of time: no need for prolonged acrobatics or showy displays of airmanship skills.

As the war went on, all sides built up their air services and so the numbers of aircraft rapidly increased. No longer did the lone pilot go off on a sortie to seek out the enemy, and as often as not, did not find anyone. Now, flights of 3-8 aircraft were quite common and almost every sortie led to the sight of an enemy formation. Both would then maneuver to achieve a superior position - and if not able to do so, they oftentimes simply chose not to engage each other. Multiple flights would be in the air and thus the combined numbers of aircraft within a given amount of airspace at any one time could be quite dramatic. As the war entered late 1917 and into 1918, there could be hundreds of aircraft in the air over active areas of battlefields on the Western Front. Thus, experienced flight leaders now had to be cautious before attacking any single enemy flight as there could be others lurking in ambush.

Leonard "Tich" Rochford of the RNAS/RAF wrote"

"I always tried to avoid prolonged involvement in 'dogfights', there being no sense in relinquishing the advantage of superior height."

Above: The end result of a successful combat at thousands of feet, would often attract a lot of attention by numerous curious people on the ground. Artist unknown

Now, a new trick evolved, A flight of several aircraft would patrol at lower altitude, inviting an attack and springing an attack from their comrades who had been sitting at a higher altitude awaiting the enemy to fall for the decoys.

A successful fighter ace and leader in the French Air Service, Capt. Albert Deullin wrote a "primer" for the French pursuit squadrons and it was translated into English by Charles Biddle so that it could be distributed to the American fighter pilots as well. One of Deullin's most sage advice in the book was:

"Attack ahead while looking to the rear."

In other words, beware of having been caught in a trap! The experienced flight leaders would be aware of such tactics and would usually be able to keep their flight out of such trouble. Still, both sides tried to engage the enemy and would do so if they felt the advantage was on their side. If not, then they flew their two hour missions over the front lines all the while jockeying for the best position and if they could not do so, then they flew back to their aerodrome and would repeat the mission again and again. If they were caught by surprise, then a quick

escape back to friendly territory was in order,

Thus, most aerial combat was more of a skirmish, a testing of the other sides capabilities and willingness to also engage.

The large release of adrenaline because of the human mind's fight or flight response to danger naturally enhanced and flavored the memoirs, and stories told by the pilots of the first world war about their combat experiences.

Even as more and more aircraft would be found in the skies over the trenches, the slow speeds and impressive turning capabilities of First World War fighter aircraft meant that as many as 30-50 aircraft could fit in a dogfight that spread itself over a 3 square mile box of airspace.

It is not that some prolonged dogfighting did not occur, it is simply that most combat resulted from a surprise diving attack by one side and desperate, quick defensive maneuvering by the other side while all combatants tried to maintain the advantage of height - failing that, most would try to dive away and escape.

As Denis Winter wrote in his book *The First of the Few*:

"Most attacks therefore took the form of an all-out dive, each pilot concentrating just on his own actions. The sensation of power diving almost precluded any other approach...gliding into the attack on a slower machine, diving behind with a climbing turn onto the tail of a faster aeroplane until the target filled the whole Aldis screen...then pressing the firing button in a succession of one- or two-second bursts."

And once a flight of aircraft descended upon the enemy, that enemy's supportive flights attempted to come to the rescue and now the dogfight was begun as the massed number of aircraft broke off into multiple individual fights. Cecil Lewis's book *Sagittarius Rising* is generally thought to be an excellent account of a pilot's experiences in the First World War. In the folio edition (1998) he attempts to describe such a dogfight:

"It would be impossible to describe the action of such a battle. A pilot, in the second between his own engagements might see a Hun diving vertically, an SE 5 on his tail, on the tail of the SE 5 another Hun, and above him another British scout. These four, plunging headlong at two hundred miles an hour, guns crackling, tracers streaming, suddenly break up. The lowest Hun plunges flaming to his death, if death had not taken him already. His victor seems to stagger, suddenly pulls out in a great leap, as a trout leaps on the end of a line, and then, turning over on his belly, swoops and spins in a dizzy falling spiral with the earth to end it...but such a glimpse, lasting perhaps ten seconds, is broken by the sharp rattle of another attack. Two machines approach head-on at breakneck speed, firing at each other, tracers whistling past each other's planes...But from above, this strange tormented circling is seen by another Hun. He drops. His gun speaks. The British machine, distracted by the sudden unseen enemy, pulls up, takes a burst through the engine, tank and body, and falls bottom uppermost down through the clouds and the deep unending desolation of the twilight sky...The fight is over! Here where guns rattled and death plucked the spirits of the valiant, this thing is now as if it had never been! The sky is busy with night, passive, superb, unheeding." (page, 122–123)

Other veteran First World War pilots have told their own versions of the dogfight, from their own perspectives and their own memories. The large release of adrenaline because of the human's intrinsic fight or flight survival mechanism naturally enhanced and even flavored these reminiscences. But there is a consistent thread to be found and much of what has been written by the pilots are of a similar vein, if not quite as eloquent as Lewis. The suddenness of the attack, the viciousness of the fight once engaged, the rapidity of the air combat and then the sudden return of quiet, the pilot finding himself in an empty sky, seemingly alone. This is the story of the dogfight, repeated again and again by those pilots who survived the prior fight and then written about by those lucky enough to survive the war.

Arthur Gould Lee wrote two well-respected books about his time in the RFC, No Parachute and Open Cockpit. He too tried his best to describe just what a First World War dogfight was like:

"We waltzed round one another as if in a vicious, unbreakable circle. First Giles, then Begbie, then a scarlet and black Hun would rush in mad confusion, each sweeping through the stringy mass of tracer bullets, making it curl up as if in a whirlpool. The barking of the machine guns was obliterated by the imminence of a terrifying collision. It was an awe-inspiring sight of hurtling machines smashing through the sky at one another which developed into a game of snap-shooting. There was no time to take aim. Try as I would, I could not bring down a single bird. Through the corner of my eye I could see my comrades taking pot shots. Suddenly I spotted a machine commencing to smoke, then burst into flames. I wondered if it was a comrade. It was. I recognized by the marking that it was poor old Begbie. A sudden feeling of sickness overcame me. Fascinated with horror I momentarily forgot to fight. Poor old Begbie had to leave us without a wave of farewell. I had a final peep at him as I flew nearby. Thank God he looked as if he were dead. There was a void in my stomach as I looked over my shoulder and saw the long black trail of smoke which marked the last fight of a beloved companion."

Arthur Gould Lee, in Open Cockpit, is likely speaking for all aviators on either side of the trenches as he summed up his thoughts as a First World War fighter pilot and the battles (dogfights) that he waged during the war:

"To be able to fight on his own was the distinguishing mark of the fighter pilot...He had to hunt for battle, and several times a day, several times an hour, might have to pass through spells of intensely lethal fighting with split-second margins between life and death that left him emotionally and physically spent...Even if he started a fight as a member of a formation, when it developed it became usually a matter of single combat. He fought not shoulder to shoulder with thousands of others but as an individual in a glove-tight aeroplane miles up in the sky, and in a dogfight, during a desperately contested duel, he could easily feel that he was fighting the war by himself."

Artists For Volume 1

The reader should remember that all artwork in the *Art of the Dogfight* series is copyrighted and cannot be copied for any reason, in any format without the permission of the artist or the appropriate copyright holder. At the end of volume 4 there is an expanded artist biography section. The page numbers to find an artist's work is for the convenience of the reader. The artwork has been permitted by the artist unless otherwise noted.

Anderson, Steve: 32, 68, 81, 84, 129, 137, 143, 153, 159, 161, 164, 175, 183

Burns, Keith: 201

Corning, Merv: 34, 42, 43, 136, 141 courtesy of Esterline's Leach International Corporation, Buena Park, CA

Cross, Roy: 131

Dennis,Peter: 37

Dietz, Jim: Cover, endpapers, 17, 18

Dillon, Andrew: 59

Evans, George: 16, 193

Faust, Charles: 202, courtesy of Willis Allen jr., Allen Airways Flying Museum

Field, James: 171, 174

Fleischer, Seweryn: 50, 56, 184

Forbes, Alan: 24

Galloway, Nixon: 196

Hardy, Wilf: 190 courtesy of Look and Learn

Karr, Robert: 108, 130

Knight, Brian: 128, 133, 194, 198, 203, courtesy of Ray Rimell-Albatros Productions Ltd.

Koike, Shigeo: 119

Martinecky, V. :63, 83 courtesy of Roden Models

Marsalko, Bill: 140

Miller, Mark: 94, 95, 200

O'Neal, Michael: 87, 122

Orpen, William: 79, 91 courtesy of IWM art collection

Phelan, Joseph: 11

Postlethwaite, Mark:127

Prejelan, Rene: 37, 58

Richards, John: 15, 65, 119, 180

Shytk, Taras: 59

Smith, Russell: 25, 150

Theobold, Tony: 54 courtesy of Group Captain W.S.O. Randle

Woodcock, Keith: 144, 157 (courtesy of Leo Opdyke)

Wyllie, W.L.: 28 courtesy of Defense Academy of the UK, art collection

Above: The aircrew of Staaken R.39 is surrounded by the ground crew for the aircraft. The commander of R.39, Hauptmann Richard von Bentivegni is in the center of the aircrew, notable for being in flight gear.

Left & Above: One of the huge 2.4 m (7 foot, 9 inch) diameter all-wood wheels made for the Poll Giant. The photos were taken at the Imperial War Museum where the wheel was once on display and is now in storage. The Poll Giant was a huge triplane bomber with ten engines that was being constructed in 1918, but was not completed by the armistice. Work stopped at war's end and the type was never completed nor flown.

Above: A Sopwith Camel of No.10 sqdn. RNAS [C flight] dives into a flight of Pfalz D.IIIa fighter of Bavarian Jasta 16 and the dogfight, chasing each other in order to get on your opponent's tail, begins. Jim Dietz

Above: Une victorie! A Spad pilot does an aerobatic exclamation over his victory, all in sight of his comrades below at their airfield. Charles Faust

55620250R00119